Hearing Beyond the Words

Emma J. Justes

Hearing

Beyond

the

Words

How to Become
a Listening Pastor

Abingdon Press

Nashville

HEARING BEYOND THE WORDS:
HOW TO BECOME A LISTENING PASTOR

Library of Congress Cataloging-in-Publication Data

Justes, Emma J., 1941-
  Hearing beyond the words : how to become a listening pastor / Emma J. Justes.
    p. cm.
  Includes bibliographical references.
  ISBN 0-687-49499-0 (pbk. : alk. paper)
  1. Pastoral theology. 2. Listening--Religious aspects--Christianity. I. Title.

  BV4319.J87 2006
  253'.7--dc22

                                                                                    2005037378

ISBN 13: 978-0-687-49499-6

08 09 10 11 12 13 14 15—10 9 8 7 6 5 4 3 2
MANUFACTURED IN THE UNITED STATES OF AMERICA

To those who have blessed me

by being students

in the courses I have taught

CONTENTS

Contents

ACKNOWLEDGMENTS

A number of years ago I came across the book *The Lost Art of Listening* by Michael P. Nichols.[1] The book awakened me to the vital role that listening plays in our lives, and particularly, in ministry. It has been a part of my teaching ever since that time. I would say that *The Lost Art of Listening* transformed my teaching of pastoral care. I owe Nichols a deep debt of gratitude for his truly wonderful, thorough, and insightful book. My journey with his book has led me to the point of writing this book especially for people in ministry and the church.

The support of my colleagues in teaching has been unflagging, especially Dr. Claude Mariottini and Dr. Douglas Sharp. The pastoral theologians of the Chicago area are a community of support and substance. Our joy in working together is an always reviving inspiration. Within this group Dr. Lee Butler has offered continuing support. Members of the staff at Northern Seminary were always ready to provide encouragement and assistance, especially Barb Wixon, Marilyn Wiley, Scott Bruce, and Dwight Hawley. Special thanks to my former colleague Dennis Groh, who has added inspiration to this work, and to my teacher James N. Lapsley for his faithful encouragement.

To the students who have studied with me over the years, I owe tremendous gratitude. You have continued to teach me as I have been in the role of teacher. You have helped me see where I need to grow and how I could do my work better, and have often brought to me the word of God. You remain in my heart and continue to prompt me toward growth. Here I name a few without trying to be inclusive of all who have been so important to me: Darlene, Patti, Gloria, Richard, Joe, Jeremy, Linda, Brenda, Theresa, John, Jeff, Gail, Roxanne, David, Ron, Fernando, Kathy, Tom, Lilliana, Gideon, Kelly, Mark, Dee. I want to include my deep gratitude to the students, Kleppie, Thami, Thabiso, Andile, Thandi, Spetla, and Viada, and colleagues I have worked with in South Africa.

The encouragement of my friends in the writing of this book has been invaluable. They witnessed the birthing of this book and stood by, listening to me through the experience. I thank especially Jacqueline Grossmann and Jeanette Repp, who enthusiastically and tirelessly read and reread portions of this manuscript even in its most ragged forms. Thanks to the people and ministers of the two churches that welcome and receive me into their families: Saint John African Methodist Episcopal Church of Aurora, Illinois, especially Pastor Jesse D. Hawkins and my beloved colleagues in ministry there, and Bethany Baptist Church of Christ in Evanston, especially Pastor Brenda J. Little.

Very special thanks to my editor, whose patience with me and faith in me have been beyond comprehension.

INTRODUCTION

The problem with listening is that it is *so easy not to do*. None of us, myself included, listen as consistently well as we might. Listening is very hard work. Listening affects all aspects of our everyday lives from the smallest one-to-one relationships to family, group, committee, congregational, and workplace relationships, as well as community, governments, and even international relationships. Listening plays a vital role in ministry in all of its forms: caregiving, education, chaplaincy, mission, administration, evangelism, and preaching. Effective ministry requires us to be able to listen well. We can't avoid the need to be able to listen *care-fully* in order to relate effectively.

"Communication" surrounds us and intrudes on our lives. People speak loudly into their cell phones in public places. Technology makes it possible for us to be in communication with people anywhere, at any time. We are deluged with communication around the clock. People "talk over" one another, even on public television. This amount of "communication" and the number of so-called talk shows would lead one to think that a lot of listening is going on. Not necessarily. Quality listening is not taking place. Outward signs do not ensure inward realities. In spite of all this connection with one another, what we are missing is *feeling connected*. We have adapted to the babble by blocking out a lot of the interference with which we are constantly bombarded. Even cutting down on this interference does not mean that we will be able to listen more deeply in today's world. It is a paradox that we are surrounded by continuous communication and yet feel disconnected, isolated, and alienated.

The cell phone commercials that feature the man who travels into every kind of setting asking, "Can you hear me now?" symbolizes for me the state of communications among those longing to be heard and the constant search for someone who will "hear me now."

We long to be connected with one another. Part of this deep longing is to be listened to, to be received by another person and *feel connected* in a way that is not superficial or minimal. Whenever I have deeply heard someone's pain or struggle and have been able to reflect that hearing back to the person effectively, the response of the person who is heard is often deep relief. When I have experienced someone deeply listening to me, I have known that response of relief and found a feeling of connection. When we are heard, we experience being "seen."

Longing for the connections, and the belonging that listening offers to us, draws us to community. Communities of faith in particular, ideally, are places where we are received and feel connected; where we are nurtured and we take the risks of growing. Being welcomed, received, and heard builds the realities of community. Within community—as part of community—people learn to speak and learn to listen. Listening is not acquired without community. Community is not created without listening.

Across cultures we cannot hear one another without struggling with the cultural differences within and surrounding what is said. Males and females have difficulty hearing one another across acquired and reinforced gender barriers.[1]

Children and their parents have great difficulties in listening to one another across generations. It is also true that pastors and parishioners do not hear one another much of the time. Nonlistening happens even in situations in which listening is *the thing that is intended*, such as in pastoral care and counseling, and for parishioners, in listening to sermons.

Assumptions we make, expectations we have, and stereotypes we hold about others and their circumstances affect how well we listen to them. Past experiences of listening and current issues with which we struggle are factors that influence our listening.

True Listening

The focus on listening here is on truly hearing another person, deeply listening. I use different phrases throughout the book to make it clear that I mean a different kind of listening—true hearing, caring listening, effective listening, pastoral listening, and healing listening. I will use such phrases to emphasize that what is being addressed is not simply the act of listening to words to which we are all accustomed. The hearing of words and the receiving of the speaker are far from being the same thing; most of our listening takes place somewhere in between these two extremes.

Teenagers today have an interesting way of expressing their understanding of what they have heard: "I feel you." The question form, which asks about whether someone has been understood (heard), is, "Do you feel me?" Or in its abbreviated forms, "You feel me?" or even, "Feel me?" These young people seem to have grasped a dimension of listening that may be less consciously available to adults. Hearing does not enter into the feeling realm unless it is truly listening. The teens' way of saying they have heard acknowledges the feeling dimension to the deep listening and authentic understanding that this book encourages.[2] The feeling content in what is spoken and what we hear may be more important than the words used for speaking.

Listening and Hospitality

Over the years, I have encouraged students to think of listening as an act of receiving—making use of the gesture of an open palm, facing up, extended as if to receive something. The use of this gesture became the impulse for me to explore the connections between hospitality and listening, since the basic movement of hospitality is also receiving.

As I have thought about listening, experienced listening and being heard, and as I have taught the importance of listening, I began to see the power of a connection between listening and hospitality. This connection was enhanced by my discovery of the great value given to hospitality in scripture. Hospitality and listening fit well together, and I believe that listening can be enhanced by some gifts found in understanding hospitality.

Because of the centrality of receiving in listening, listening can be understood as an act of hospitality. Listening, like hospitality, not only involves receiving another person, but includes being welcoming and open to the speaker who is in our presence. Ability to listen is rooted in the *person* or character of the listener, as is hospitality.

Neither listening nor hospitality is lodged solely in *practice*, but each is also a matter of *being*. Listening is not a matter of precise procedure, nor is it entirely a matter of "Whoever has ears let them hear."[3] As this saying indicates on the surface, there is a need for ears in order to hear.

However, having ears doesn't always mean we hear.[4] "Whoever has ears" otherwise may mean "those who welcome me and my words *into* their lives," or "those who recognize the true meaning of what is said and welcome it." Receiving, whether in the practice of hospitality or in listening, does not happen with closed hands, crossed arms, or a clenched heart. Being able to receive another with listening hospitality requires willingness and ability *to be open to the other*—with hands, arms, and hearts open and ready to receive.

A Story of Missing Listening

A woman came to my house weekly over a period of months. This woman never invited me to tell her about myself, or left me any openings in which to do so. I would listen as she struggled to bring the gospel, as she understood it, to me and convince me of the correctness of her faith and the importance of my accepting it. She had no idea who I was or what I already knew about God or already believed. I wanted to see if she would ever ask.

Finally we met under other circumstances and she discovered that I was a seminary professor. She didn't return to our house. I did not remain silent about myself to embarrass her or in any way diminish her faith. I didn't intend to make this experience an experiment. It was only after many visits that it dawned on me that her approach was clearly general and did not include the specifics of my life and me. I have long believed what Carroll Wise said in defining pastoral care, which points toward the particularity of the individual. I realized that I was curious about what this woman brought and was impressed with her diligence and enthusiasm, but I did not feel "touched." What I suspect is that my visitor made assumptions about me and who I was, and from these assumptions she brought her message. This visitor helped me see how very important listening is, before evangelism.

The generalized approach taken by my visitor is much like the approach of the pastor who described a hospital visit, "I offered some words of comfort and then left." Maybe those same "words of comfort" had been offered to every hospitalized parishioner in that pastor's ministry experience. Within failures to listen are assumptions about what people "need," which always are just that—assumptions.

The Heart of Caring Ministries

We identify ourselves as people who "love to tell the story," which was clearly my visitor's approach. It is important to remember that in order to tell the story effectively, we need to know the person to whom we tell the story—to have some sense of where that person is on their faith journey. This cannot be discovered apart from listening. Carroll Wise's definition of pastoral care as communicating the gospel to persons at the point of their need has been a staple in my teaching of pastoral care.[5] If we are to effectively provide pastoral care, it becomes necessary to first know what a person's point of need happens to be. Otherwise, care becomes a generalized shot in the dark with no target and no consideration of the individual to whom care is being offered.

Pastoral Listening

Pastoral listening takes place in a variety of contexts. First, pastoral listening occurs in the context of all of the functions of ministry, which are located in the contexts of a wide variety of human communities. Pastoral listening takes place in the context of listening to God and of God listening to us.

In *every* area of ministry careful listening is a key to effective ministry. Preaching may *seem* to be an exception to this claim, but in order to bring the Word of God to the people of God it is necessary to know where the people of God are at this time and in this place. Listening to the people is a prelude to preaching. The preaching pastor who knows the people to whom she or he brings the message of the sermon, knows how to address it to these particular people. The gospel is not generic, but connects with people in particular ways as it relates to their lives. Hearing the people is the way they are known; their struggles, pains, and needs are revealed in listening to them.

Not Being Heard

As we think about listening and strive to improve our listening, it is necessary to give some attention to the experience of *not being heard*. It is important to recognize what other persons experience when we are not listening to them. When we experience the frustration of feeling we are not being heard, we seldom break the rules of politeness and challenge the one who is merely *seeming* to listen to us. As speakers we are able to recognize nonlistening even when it is not so obviously conveyed as with a glance at a watch, wandering eyes, or even yawns.

We can *sense* when another is not listening to us. We can experience this even when there are the signals to the contrary, such as sustained eye contact, repeated nods, or verbal affirmations like "uh huh" or "I see." We go on speaking even when we have a sense that we are not being heard. Perhaps we keep talking with the hope that what we sense and suspect is wrong and that indeed we are being heard. Or we continue to speak with the hope that something will catch the listener's attention.

Awareness of the experience of those who speak to us and are not heard is important for encouraging our efforts to become the best listeners we can be. Remember, if you are able to sense that someone is not listening to you, speakers will be able to sense when you are not listening to them.

Levels of Listening

Even though we all come with different levels of listening abilities, all of us can improve our listening skills. As ministers we want to be able to evaluate our listening—how are we doing as listeners? We also want to be able to tell whether someone to whom we are listening actually experiences being heard. This book is written with the recognition that we do not come with the same degree of listening skills; nor do we, whatever our skill levels, listen with the same degree of focus all of the time. The poorest listener may have brilliant moments when her or his attention is captured and held rapt. The whole message is heard loud and clear, and appropriate response is given.

The best of listeners, however, will have moments of stress or distraction that draw them away from their usual gifts in listening and into moments of, perhaps, more self-preoccupation. Being a consistently effective listener includes moments in which we lapse into poor listening. Being an effective listener includes learning how to recover and return to the person we are failing or have failed to hear, to listen with renewed attention. As we examine our own listening, we do well to have compassion for ourselves as listeners, recognizing our personal and ministry contexts that influence our listening.

Overview

This book is intended for use as a workbook for seminary classes in areas of pastoral care and counseling. But it is not intended only for the audience of the seminary class, since it is designed so that it also can be used by individuals or by any groups in the church interested in improving their listening abilities. It will be helpful not only to pastors, but also to groups within a congregation or parish who want to do their work together more effectively: church boards or committees, for example. The exercises are easily adaptable for a variety of church and personal uses.

Before we get into the first chapter of the book, I offer the reader some exercises intended to prepare readers for being ready to listen. These are found within the Introduction in a section called "Exercises to Get Started." The first chapter brings us to a discussion of foundations for listening and an understanding of the importance of hospitality in the Jewish and Christian faith traditions. Qualities found in hospitality form the basis for each of the following chapters. Chapter 2 discusses what is necessary in order to prepare to listen effectively. Chapter 3 encourages listening to what is not actually being said, in receiving physical communications that may significantly alter what is heard. Often feelings are not named and yet can be seen as the person speaks. The last two chapters present concerns about the limits of the listening pastor and the gift of listening for God as one listens to others.

We will look at ways to improve listening skills using focus questions and exercises related to each chapter. Following each chapter there are focus questions. These questions encourage further consideration and application of that which was presented in the chapter. The exercises following each chapter (and this introduction) are designed to increase one's awareness of one's listening effectiveness and discover barriers to one's hearing as ways to improve one's listening skills. There is an additional short section at the end of the book that includes more skill-building exercises. Readers also are encouraged to keep a listening journal to use for recording progress and growth in listening discoveries and skills. The journal can provide a place to keep track of self-developed programs designed for diminishing barriers to listening. The journal can also be a place to write prayers that you use for preparing yourself for listening—prayers for yourself, your focus and clarity, and prayers for those you visit. Some people find journal keeping to be burdensome;

others have discovered that tracking oneself can be of value. Try it. You may like it.

Some of the exercises provide a place for feedback from those to whom you listen as a way to further assess your self-perceptions. The exercises offer opportunities to observe the listening of others and intentionally focus on how it feels to be "half listened to." The chapters and exercises take readers through stages toward more effective listening, with the recognition that growth in effective listening is a lifelong process that continues to be a challenge.

Introductory Exercise: Noticing When You Are Heard

Intuitively, you know when you are not being heard. Those with preaching experience can observe the congregation even while preaching a sermon and notice those who at least appear attentive. (They may not realize that you can notice.) What is it in their demeanor that tells you they hear the meaning of what you are saying? Nods of heads, smiles, an attitude of attentiveness, looking at you with apparent focus? In the African American church there are signs that are verbalized in amens, in encouraging exclamations such as "Preach!" or in physical signs of hands raised in agreement, or persons standing up. These are signs that tell us that we are being heard as we speak. Culture makes a difference in the ways people show attentiveness. Eye contact, for example, is considered rude rather than attentive in some cultures.

We also detect signs of nonlistening in bored expressions and apparent nonattentiveness—looking elsewhere, sleeping, reading, appearing obviously distracted.[6] We have ways of knowing when others do not listen to us. Being in the position of speaking to a group of people is only illustrative. These comments apply in one-to-one conversations as well. Often we do not tune in to this information because we do not want it to be distracting. More important, we do not want to be hurt. We do not want to admit to ourselves that the other(s) are not listening.

The Exercise

Spend a designated period of time—a few days, a week (*not* just a few hours)—that will span a variety of contacts with other persons. Set your time boundaries. Observe how others listen to you. Be especially aware of those times when others convey that they *are not* listening. At those points focus on *what it is that tells you the person is not listening.* Is it glazed-over eyes or a fixed facial expression? Is it smiling when you speak of a tragedy? Something in their manner tells you that he or she "checked out." Identify what it is that tells you the person is not listening, even if you feel you are just guessing.

The Written Assignment

Keep a list of descriptions of what signaled you that another person was not hearing you. Be aware that family members may be the best subjects for this exercise. For your own benefit you might also keep notes of those moments when someone was hearing you and how you knew this was the case. This exercise is a good place to make use of keeping a listening journal. Use your list to write in essay form what you have learned about listening from this exercise. What were the signs you noticed? What were the feelings you noticed? *This is an exercise about you and your self-awareness.* Keep this as your focus.

This information that enables you to know when someone is or isn't listening to you is *information you already have internally.* All of us tend to fail to make use of it as a way to improve our own listening. This is your opportunity to discover and make use of what you already know.

Exercises to Get Started

Nonverbal Communications

This exercise offers an opportunity to practice your skills in attending to nonverbal communications. Turn off the sound on the television and watch people who are speaking. This might be watching anything from a politician to a television evangelist, a sitcom or portion of a movie. What is your response to the nonverbal signals you "hear" from facial expressions, gestures, and so forth? What is the speaker communicating without the benefit of the sound? It might be interesting to tape the same segment you are watching and evaluating and later play it back with sound. How do the messages from the nonverbal and the sound version coordinate?

Becoming Open to Listening

The aim of this exercise is to prepare you for moments when receiving what is said may be increasingly difficult. By practicing listening in a non-threatening setting, you can develop "muscles" for being able to welcome and receive when it is difficult to do so. Settle somewhere where you can be comfortable, relaxed, and undisturbed. Select some enjoyable music. Listen to the music and make an effort to open yourself to receive the music. Do more than your accustomed listening. Welcome the music and receive it; be attentive to it; give it a place in your self. Keep paying attention to your quality of listening. How hospitable are you being to the music?

Choosing a Place to Grow

Pick a subject that you know little or nothing about but that may just be an issue you need to listen to in your ministry. Identify the source of your interest in this subject. What draws you to choose this particular subject? Make a note of what you discover about making this choice. Develop a plan for how you will learn about the subject. Put your plan in writing (in your journal) and follow through on it. This kind of plan could be a short-term plan or a long-term plan that might mean several years of study (not full time). As you learn more about the subject make some notes on your progress in feelings and attitudes about the subject. Place yourself in a context in which you will be able to have experiences related to the subject. For example, if you know little about prison life, arrange to visit a prison. This could be arranged through church groups that have programs of prison visitation or through a prison chaplain. If you know little about domestic violence, contact a shelter for battered women to arrange to speak with one of the staff. (For the sake of the safety of the women at the shelter, you probably will not be allowed to visit the shelter or speak with the women there.) Another option would be to locate an *open* Alcoholics Anonymous meeting to attend as an observer. Be certain it is an open meeting.

Trusting in Vulnerability

With a partner, arrange to take a walk guided by your partner while you wear a blindfold. The objective of this exercise is to work toward being more comfortable with being vulnerable. When you are guided by someone else and not able to see for yourself where you are going and whether you are safe, feelings of vulnerability emerge. There is some similarity between the experience of this exercise and being willing to let the speaker take you where she or he might choose rather than following your guidance through questions, for example. You might experience resistance to trusting your partner, just as you would experience resistance to allowing the speaker to lead the conversation.

You and your partner could reverse roles and you take the lead in guiding your blindfolded partner around. The guide should not limit the trip you take to a smooth route, but allow the partner to encounter stairs, rocky paths, twists and turns. The partner who is blindfolded should not be able to see around the blindfold or the purpose of the experience is lost.

In your journal write briefly about your experience of being led around and being vulnerable to the leading of your partner. Also write about your feelings in being the one who is the leader, on whom your partner relies for a safe journey. You might want to share your reflections with your partner.

Testing Your Inner Senses

This exercise requires at least one partner and can be enhanced by having several partners in succession. Select people who differ in gender, height, race, or culture from you and from one another, in addition to selecting one who is most like you.

This is a simple exercise that involves merely walking toward one another. This exercise enables the participants to discover the inner sense they have about their own personal space and to evaluate their ability to sense and respect the space of each partner. The space you need is likely to vary from one partner to another (if they are different from one another).

Here are the specifications: You are to walk toward one another, looking at one another until you reach a zone of discomfort. When you feel you have gotten too close, back up and adjust your distance. You and your partner will have to work together on this, with each of you deciding what distance feels comfortable to you. It may be that your partner and you do not find a distance that is agreeable to both of you. How do you work out a compromise? The distance one finds comfortable depends on one's life experiences, culture, size in relation to the partner, and the gender and race of the partner in relation to yours. There is no judgment involved in the distance each partner elicits.

You may discover that if you stand side by side rather than face-to-face, you will be able to feel comfortable with much less distance between you. Notice and write about your experience of your inner sense of the space you need and how it has differed with different partners. This sense of space is the same kind of sense you have about other issues in your experience of listening. Perhaps this exercise can help you trust what you sense. Take time to discuss the experiences with your partners.

CHAPTER ONE

LISTENING AS CHRISTIAN HOSPITALITY

Introduction

The Scriptures use many different forms of the words listen, listened, hear, and heard. I located almost fifteen hundred references. The phrase often repeated to the people of Israel, "Hear, O Israel . . ." alerted the people to listen, to attend to the important words that would follow. The prophetic tradition that declared, "Thus says the Lord," emphasized the act of listening as the people were called to attention with these introductory words. In the ministry of Jesus, his parables frequently ended with the phrase, "Let whoever has ears to hear listen." How can we, then, ignore the importance of listening?

Whereas we have a strong scriptural tradition that emphasizes listening and hearing, I turn to the biblical image of hospitality for a theological grounding of the practice of listening, because hospitality bespeaks the kind of relationship best suited for listening and hearing. As I have worked with listening I have seen that there are some clear commonalities between hospitality and listening. Both deserve more importance in ministry. Therefore, in this chapter we will examine selected passages of scripture that deal with hospitality in order to explore how it can enrich our understanding and practice of listening.

The qualities required in hospitality—its essence—I propose are also those elements that are necessary for effective listening. An examination of hospitality gives us a deeper, more nuanced understanding of listening. My purpose in exploring the relationship between hospitality and listening, at its heart, is to enable, encourage, and support the practice of more effective listening.

This chapter explores the meaning and practice of hospitality in a Christian context, identifying its implications for listening to one another. My hope is that seeing the connections and gaining greater understanding of hospitality will enhance the practice of listening on the part of those in ministry.

So what can we learn from an understanding of hospitality that will help us move toward better listening? Throughout this chapter I invite you to keep listening in mind as we discover more about hospitality. What we discover here about hospitality will lead to the practice of more effective listening.

A Scriptural Base for Hospitality

It took many years of reading the Bible before I began to become aware of the importance of hospitality in its message. Now I find it difficult to miss the significance of hospitality as I read the Scriptures. A familiar and foundational story of hospitality from the Scripture is found in the eighteenth chapter of Genesis. The story begins when three strangers arrive at the tent of Abraham and Sarah in the desert.

Dr. Dennis Groh describes the appropriate approach to a tent in the desert. Recognizing that the desert is itself less than hospitable, hospitality among those who travel the desert becomes extremely important. The one who approaches another's tent is required to sit at a distance from the tent and wait to be noticed. To approach unacknowledged can be seen as a threatening gesture. Once acknowledged, the host goes out to welcome the strangers who are then free to approach the tent.[1] Readers of Genesis 18 would benefit from holding this context in mind. Hospitality is culturally sensitive, which makes it important to be aware of the context in which hospitality is being experienced or observed.

In Genesis 18 Abraham noticed three men standing in the desert.[2] Abraham ran to greet them (v. 2). He welcomed the men to his tent and offered them water to wash with. Abraham was insistent in encouraging them to accept his hospitality and sensitive in acknowledging that they were on a journey and he did not intend to detain them once they were

2

refreshed (vv. 4-5). Sarah and their servants were enlisted to join in the quick preparation of a feast for these guests. The best flour and a plump calf were chosen to serve these strangers in the desert (vv. 6-8).

The guests, true to hospitality's form, offered their hosts something before leaving. They left the childless couple, well into old age, the promise that not only would the visitors return, but that Abraham and Sarah were still going to be parents (vv. 10-11). One of the men said that by the next year Sarah would be the mother of a son, which would fulfill the promise God had made to Abraham many years earlier. The visitors were offered excellent hospitality and they responded with a "hostess gift" of inestimable worth. This story of Abraham and Sarah is illustrative of a pervasive biblical attitude toward hospitality that we see again and again. Hospitality is required and hospitality is rewarded.

The story continued when the visitors left and Abraham walked a distance with them (v. 16). The Lord, who was entertained by Abraham and Sarah on this occasion, was on the way to Sodom in order to see firsthand whether the "outcry against Sodom" warranted its destruction for its wickedness (vv. 20-21). This visitor hung back, talking with Abraham, as Abraham negotiated with him to save the city from destruction. Abraham challenged the Lord's sense of justice in destroying any people in the city who were righteous along with those who were wicked (vv. 23-25). The Lord graciously agreed to each of the lowered stakes offered until Abraham got the Lord to agree that for the sake of ten righteous people Sodom would not be destroyed (vv. 24-32). I often wonder what the Lord would have done if Abraham's asking got down to one person.

When the strangers arrived in Sodom (there were then only two), Lot insisted that they accept his hospitality for the night, even though they resisted. Although he only offered water to wash their feet and a night's lodging, he provided for them a fine feast (19:2-4). After Lot and his guests had eaten, the men of the city, acting in stark contrast to Lot's hospitality, demanded that Lot send the strangers out in order that they "may know them"(v. 5). Lot took his role as host so seriously that he offered to protect his guests by handing over his own virgin daughters to the mob (v. 8).[3] The purposes of the mob were thwarted with the help of the strangers, who set out a plan for rescuing Lot and his family from the sure destruction that would befall Sodom (vv. 9-17).

In becoming a host to the strangers, Lot had put himself in the role of protecting his guests. This is a further obligation of hospitality. Here the story of Lot's hospitality differs from the story of Abraham and Sarah. In

Lot's story it became necessary for Lot, as host, to protect his guests, a problem Abraham and Sarah did not face.

The guests, in turn, as they did with Abraham and Sarah, had something of significance to offer Lot and his household. Lot acted to protect his guests, and the guests turned out to be instrumental in the salvation of his family in their rescue.

The roles tend to turn around guest-to-host and host-to-guest when we examine hospitality. The visitor/guest comes with something significant to offer, not with empty hands. The guest comes with a need (for food, shelter, rest), but is not without a blessing to give. The host may anticipate that something will be received from the visitor, but there is no way to know what to expect. The host knows for sure that the household *will be affected by guests* who enter—something, or much, will change.

Central to this second story of hospitality is the bold contrast between the practice of hospitality and the absence of hospitality. Lot was the one who held to and practiced the value of hospitality. The people of Sodom, in their blatant hostility toward strangers, were destroyed for their lack of hospitality—indeed, their *hostility* toward *hospitality*. Every man of the city, "both young and old, all the people to the last man," participated in the mob that demanded that the strangers be handed over to them; so Abraham's bargain with the Lord to save Sodom for the sake of ten who were righteous was off. Sodom would not be spared. However, the rescue of Lot and his family members who consented to go with him seems to affirm the upholding of God's justice. Where there was true hospitality, in Lot's household, the people were spared.

From the beginning of the story of the people of Israel, hospitality is a core value. Their experiences of being strangers in foreign lands, being slaves in Egypt, and wandering in the desert gave the people a clear sense of the value of hospitality. Being hospitable became a sign of being faithful. The tradition of referring to those who are faithful to God as sons and daughters of Abraham points back to the centrality of this story to the people of Israel.

New Testament

When we turn to the New Testament we find vivid messages about hospitality. I have selected a few to examine here; primarily my focus will be on the story of the "sinful" woman in Luke, chapter seven. This story began when Jesus was invited to the home of a Pharisee to eat. We see similar qualities of hospitality in this very different story.

The Outrageous Host

When we read descriptions of biblical events we tend to picture them through our modern-day experience. We would see Jesus coming to the house of the Pharisee, Simon, joining others who were invited, and taking a chair at a table. We must allow ourselves to see where there are differences that do not match our assumptions if we are to come closer to understanding the meaning of the passage. William Herzog offers this description:

> Kenneth Bailey has argued that the meal held in Simon's house was a public occasion. Although not everyone was invited to recline at table with the supposedly honored guest, everyone was invited to sit around the wall of the *triclinium* (dining room) and listen to the Pharisees discuss Torah with their visitor.[4]

The scene, thus interpreted, relies on seeing the function of the home of the Pharisee as a place where the synagogue could be extended, where the people could gather to listen to the study and discussion of Torah between invited guests and the Pharisees.[5] With this understanding, we might see Jesus' easy question to Simon as kicking off the discussion and teaching.

What a different picture we get when we add all the villagers who sit around the wall observing the events and listening to what is said. The scene changes when we take away the chairs to envision invited guests reclining at the table. We have to struggle to picture the scene as it was, with Jesus lying facing the table with his feet stretched out toward the wall of the room.[6] This arrangement accounts for the scriptural description of the woman's location in relation to Jesus, "She stood *behind him* at his feet" (v. 38). Picturing the event from our context, with Jesus seated at the table in a chair, makes this a puzzling image, and the woman a bit of a contortionist.

Because Jesus was an honored guest, being invited to eat at the table, it was customary that he would be shown certain acts of hospitality as he arrived. Simon's neglect of these duties of hospitality did not go unnoticed. In failing to honor Jesus with required expressions of hospitality, Simon's behavior was an insult to Jesus.[7] Other guests who may already have been present and those who were sitting around the walls would have noticed the failure of Simon to act as host to Jesus. The woman could have been one of these witnesses or perhaps she could have heard from someone who was there at the time when Jesus arrived.

The sinful (unclean) woman reached out to Jesus from her place by the wall and began to kiss and bathe his feet with ointment and her tears, and then dry his feet with her hair (vv. 37-38). Every one of her actions reverses one of the insults that Simon has inflicted on Jesus.[8] Her behavior was outrageous. She not only touched Jesus' feet, but she had let her hair down in public, which was culturally prohibited. Since the Pharisees considered her unclean , her touch made Jesus unclean in their eyes. The host of this event saw the attention Jesus was receiving as reflecting badly on Jesus. He muttered to himself that if Jesus were truly a prophet he would know what kind of woman she was and would not let her touch him (v. 39).

Jesus responded to his host's criticism with a simple story about a creditor and two debtors, each forgiven of their debts. Jesus asked Simon, the Pharisee, an easy question: Which debtor would love the creditor more? Simon answered that the one whose debt was greater would love the creditor more. After affirming the answer Simon gave (vv. 40-43), Jesus brought the point of the story home and called to Simon's attention Simon's serious neglect of the requirements of hospitality.[9] Jesus said:

> Do you see this woman? I entered your house; you gave me no water for my feet, but she has bathed my feet with her tears and dried them with her hair. You gave me no kiss, but from the time I came in she has not stopped kissing my feet. You did not anoint my head with oil, but she has anointed my feet with ointment. Therefore, I tell you, her sins, which were many, have been forgiven; hence she has shown great love. But the one to whom little is forgiven, loves little. (vv. 44-47)

The appreciation Jesus expressed for hospitality was clear. Simon hadn't even seen the connection between his lack of hospitality and the woman's generous hospitality. Simon had no right to judge the woman when he had neglected to offer Jesus, his guest, the very basic hospitality that was expected. The sinful woman "showed up" the righteous Pharisee, and did so in his own home. Her hospitality offered Jesus the very basics that Simon had neglected to give to Jesus as his guest. She might not have kept all of the laws of the Torah, but she knew and demonstrated what truly counted.

Hospitality for Jesus

In Matthew we see further support for the very high importance given to hospitality in the Christian faith. Jesus described the final judgment. His description of separating out those who are blessed by God reflects the very basis for receiving blessings as acts of hospitality.

> ". . . for I was hungry and you gave me food, I was thirsty and you gave me something to drink, I was a stranger and you welcomed me, I was naked and you gave me clothing, I was sick and you took care of me, I was in prison and you visited me." Then the righteous will answer him, "Lord, when was it that we saw you hungry and gave you food, or thirsty and gave you something to drink? And when was it we saw you a stranger and welcomed you, or naked and gave you clothing? And when was it that we saw you sick or in prison and visited you?" And the king will answer them, "Truly I tell you, just as you did it to one of the least of these who are members of my family, you did it to me." (Matt. 25:35-40)

Hospitality stands out as a crucial requirement for those who would follow Jesus. There is a surprise in this passage that we cannot miss. Here is another turnabout in which *Jesus becomes the guest* when we offer hospitality to one who is in need. What is the message here about hospitality?

We continue by examining the passages presented to discover some essential elements of hospitality. As we do so, we begin to create the foundation for the subsequent chapters of this book in which the connections between hospitality and listening will be defined. Each of the characteristics or elements—vulnerability, humility, thoughtful availability, and reciprocity—which can be seen as central to the practice of hospitality, is also central to the practice of effective listening. Seeing them through the eyes of valued hospitality, we discover these same values to be present in listening, as well.

The Four Core Qualities of Hospitality

Vulnerability

We see from the stories of Abraham and Sarah and Lot that offering hospitality involves vulnerability. Abraham and Lot were quick and persistent in inviting strangers into their homes. We might assume that they shrewdly evaluated the strangers or saw some god/angel likeness in their demeanor, but the texts do not make this clear. Both Abraham and Lot greeted the strange men by bowing down to the ground and referring to them as lords. Lot and Abraham each referred to himself as "your servant." Such greetings were a show of respect and not greetings reserved just for God or angels.

Lot and his family became vulnerable, facing danger because of the hospitality Lot offered to the strangers. His invitation and welcome placed him in a threatened position as their host. The danger was not from the strangers themselves, but from the response of the people of the city to the presence of the strangers and to Lot's having offered them hospitality.

Perhaps Lot had himself experienced the antihospitable attitude of the people of Sodom. The men who came to take the strangers said of Lot, "This fellow came here as an alien, and he would play the judge!" (Genesis 19:9). Obviously, he had not been welcomed as "one of them" by the people of Sodom. His experience prior to this particular evening might have warned Lot that the strangers would be treated badly if they remained in the square, and his invitation and welcome could have been extended with full awareness of the danger it might pose to him and to his family. As a "son of Abraham" Lot chose to do what was right. Hospitality can bring with it vulnerability to danger.

Danger such as Lot faced in offering hospitality is seen throughout history. People in danger are welcomed into homes even when the hosts recognize that the danger their guests face is likely to come on them. In Germany during the Holocaust, many Christians became traditionally the "sons and daughters of Abraham" when they took in and hid Jews whose lives were endangered. During slavery in America, persons who opened their homes to runaways and prepared their way on the Underground Railroad risked their own safety to enable slaves to travel toward freedom. In just these two examples we can see the amazing power of hospitality to draw people into danger in order to do what is expected by their faith—or just to do what they know is right.

We see another image of vulnerability in the woman who risked to offer Jesus hospitality. She reversed the indignity offered to Jesus by the Pharisee who was the host. She behaved outrageously. She placed herself at risk to offer the honor she was able to provide to one she very obviously saw as worthy of the deepest kind of hospitality possible. She made a spectacle of herself by her behavior. Her behavior also made a spectacle of Simon, the host. I envision the sneer on Simon's face as he watched her, seeing only her sinfulness, without recognizing that this woman was out-doing him in hospitality. She subjected herself to being seen as offensive by everyone present (except Jesus, of course). Her courage is impressive.

When we open our doors to strangers, we put ourselves and our loved ones at risk. When we open a tent flap, a door, or our heart to someone else, there is the potential of being hurt. We realize that there's a risk in being vulnerable. Hospitality (and the vulnerability it involves) does not happen without our openness to another—opening up to their presence and the impact it may have on our lives.

Sometimes it seems in America today we have a great emphasis on the fears that surround our lives. Children are warned not to speak to strangers. "Stranger danger" is involved when we are open to others whom we do not know well.[10] Some persons who are strangers come with a friendly appear-ance and behavior that causes us not to identify them as strangers. (It has been shown that children are particularly vulnerable to friendly *appearing* strangers.) We cannot look at a person we do not know and reliably eval-uate whether they are a threat or not. In offering hospitality, there are risks involved. Being open in any way makes us vulnerable.

Vulnerability takes other forms. When someone enters with need, we wonder whether their needs are genuine. We may worry about how we will be able to respond. We may be concerned about being found lacking in what they need from us and that we would fail in some way at hospi-tality. These possibilities also cause feelings of vulnerability. All of these feelings of vulnerability emerge beyond being wary about the stranger's intentions. Opening the door to the safety of our home ushers in vulner-ability, for the one opening the door and for those who would enter as guests. Vulnerability, as we are open to others, opens us up to criticism, which we do not become vulnerable to when we remain closed.

Vulnerability is not for hosts alone. Guests also place themselves in positions of vulnerability when they accept the hospitality offered to them. How can they be sure that what is being offered will be what they actually will receive? Or will they be endangered by the one offering hos-pitality? Will accepting an invitation prove to be safe? In addition, when one receives hospitality, the one who is the guest may feel that there is a demand for repayment through a return invitation, for example. We have seen that hospitality is rewarded, but a sense of obligation does not seem to fit with a true understanding of hospitality. Hospitality as it is offered to those in need may involve guests who are not able to repay in a traditional sense.

Part of our struggle with feeling vulnerable comes from the recognition that being vulnerable may bring change. The lives of all of the biblical characters we have seen were dramatically changed. Abraham and Sarah became parents in their old age. Lot's family was rescued from their destroyed city and forced to relocate. The gracious woman in Luke experienced forgiveness and salvation. These are incredible life changes. We see again that vulnerability requires great courage. To face the risk of the unknown; to face the inevitability of change in one's life; and to do so freely is a challenge for any of us in our bravery quotient.

Humility

As we think about humility in hospitality, keep in mind that the discussion here is leading us to a fresh look at listening. What we see here about hospitality, we will later see as true about listening.

Offering hospitality involves humility on the part of both the host and the guest. In acts of hospitality the primary focus is on the one in need who will become the guest and recipient of the hospitality. By being the guest, humility is already part of the package. The guest is the one in need and the host is the one who has something the guest needs.

The host who welcomes the guest with arrogance and showiness violates the true nature of hospitality, and may be satisfying her or his need to receive appreciation from others. "Look! What a fine host!" is not the response one seeks when offering true hospitality. Hospitality is done with quietness and humility. Humility is in the recognition that what I have to offer is limited, and I recognize that even as a generous host I do not have everything my guests might need—or even everything I need myself.

Abraham and Sarah had long waited for the heir promised by God. They had given up on the promise without losing their faithfulness. Sarah's laughter when she hears the guests renew the promise reflects her long-past-hope condition. These two were clearly people standing in need even as they opened their tent to strangers in the desert. As people in need they also recognized that they had something to offer and that the strangers, at this point in time, needed what they could offer.

Abraham offered his guests a *morsel* of bread and a *little* water to wash their feet, and acknowledged that they would, of course, want to move on to their destination without further ado after they had rested and had a bit of nourishment. He was the very model of humility. The guests accepted his hospitality. Then Abraham burst into action *rushing* to get

Sarah to make the bread *quickly* (from the *best* flour), *running* to get the best calf and have it prepared *hastily*.

The first offerings of a brief rest, a bit of bread, and a little water to wash with were greatly diminished, humble gestures, meant to downplay the efforts required to provide hospitality. To make the guests feel that their hosts had been "put upon" or "put out" in offering hospitality would have been in poor taste. It would have been extremely inappropriate for Abraham and Sarah to brag about what a feast they would offer their guests, if their guests stopped by. Their rush to get things underway, however, demonstrated their willingness to set themselves aside for the sake of focus on their guests and emphasized the importance of the guests—signs of humility.

Following the model of Abraham and Sarah, Lot also downplayed what he would provide for the guests. Both Abraham and Lot refer to the strangers as "Lord" and to themselves as their servants. The image of service in the context of hospitality is quite appropriate. The one who offers hospitality places him or herself in a role of *servant* to the guest, by some cultural standards a further dimension of humility.

In contrast, Simon the Pharisee's neglect of offering hospitality to Jesus was a dramatic *failure of humility*. Simon seems to have been all about outdoing Jesus (keep in mind the increasing numbers who were following Jesus). Inviting Jesus to come to his home, enjoy a meal, and enter into the theological discussion was designed to show Jesus up for the false prophet Simon thought him to be.

The woman, instead, demonstrated extreme humility, anointing and weeping on Jesus' feet, kissing his feet and wiping them with what she had available, her hair. This is what she had to offer and she was willing to do so even though she knew that the people present at the banquet would look down on her and shun her. She risked degradation in order to be the one to offer Jesus the hospitality that both society and religion demanded.

In both the stories of Lot and of Jesus at Simon's house we have failures of hospitality that are in extreme contrast to the true hospitality offered by the heroes of the stories. Where the community should have been participating in offering hospitality to strangers, it offered instead threat to their lives. Where Simon should have offered Jesus the hospitality due to a prominent guest, the woman considered unclean offered hospitality.

We cannot presume that hospitality is limitless. The guest who comes and stays forever, the visitor who rudely intrudes on the family that has offered hospitality, are presumptuous and low on awareness as well as on humility. When hospitality is offered—offered with humility—it is done with a sense of one's limitations and recognition of the limitations of the others involved—family members and the guests who have been received. Abraham's welcome to the strangers in the desert was given with recognition that they were on a journey and that he did not intend to detain them. He was there to offer them refreshment, and they were free to pursue their journey. The recognition of limitations of what the guests might want is part of hospitality. Even when they are urged to accept the hospitality offered, they are not diverted from the demands of their own lives.

There would be no need for hospitality if everyone could live independently under all circumstances without the presence, care, or service of others. This being the case, there would no longer be any humility, either. Humility is recognition that one has limits, and includes awareness of the limitations of others and the appropriate boundaries within which we function.

Humility recognizes that hospitality is not limitless. It has boundaries. Humility embraces an awareness of one's limitations, shortcomings, and flaws. It includes a sense of an appropriate self-assessment—truly seeing oneself *in perspective* as neither "all that" nor "not at all." Humility allows one to offer service to another through hospitality and to do so without devaluing oneself. Humility, rather than diminishing oneself, offers a "right way" of seeing oneself that is required for providing appropriate hospitality. Why aren't we more consistently able to look at ourselves with this realistic perspective—seeing both who we are and who we are not, and at the same time realizing our place in God's family?

Thoughtful Availability

"Thoughtful availability," Dennis Groh's descriptive phrase for Abraham's standing by under the tree while his guests ate, seems very applicable to an understanding of the character of hospitality.[11] Our stance as listeners will draw on this image of thoughtful availability. The image of thoughtful availability reminds me of the host who stands by, attentive to the needs of the guest, jumping up from the table to refill a water glass when it is empty, inquiring whether the guest has had enough to eat or whether she would "Like a little more . . . ?"

The image of thoughtful availability reminds me of servers in elegant restaurants, present to every need of the guests, anticipating what they will want or need next—alert to serve. The role of being a servant may be downplayed as insignificant or humiliating, but it is a role we take on when we act to offer hospitality. Groh further describes his concept, "To be a host like Abraham is to make one's personal presence available to the guest—to form a receptive alliance with the guest."[12] "At your service" seems like an appropriate phrase to reflect thoughtful availability.

My colleague Dr. Roland Kuhl proposes a shift from understanding ministry by using a model of leadership more prominent in the business world, to understanding ministry by using a model of servantship.[13] His view aligns with the view of hospitality I present here. He points out that Jesus offered us the basis for the image of ministry as servantship in John 13:14-15: "So if I, your Lord and Teacher, have washed your feet, you also ought to wash one another's feet. For I have set you an example, that you also should do as I have done to you." Far from being demeaning, the role of servant and service to one another is honored by Jesus in word and deed.

Thoughtful availability means going beyond the needs for food and drink, to being alert to other needs for the comfort of the guest. This is clearly a characteristic that was missing from Simon. He failed to give his focus to Jesus as his guest in the way Groh describes hospitality; instead his focus on Jesus revealed a defensive stance. Simon thought to himself that Jesus was certainly not "all that." He couldn't possibly be the prophet some claimed he was. Now Simon had the evidence. If Jesus were a prophet, surely he would have agreed with Simon's view of the woman, and Jesus would not have allowed her to fawn over him, actually touching him.

Simon's attention directed toward Jesus was so intent on and captive to his defensiveness that it was very far from being thoughtful availability. Simon's disregard of offering Jesus the required rituals of hospitality demonstrated that he was ready to downgrade Jesus from any prophet status even before the thoughtful woman touched him. Simon's hospitality (inviting Jesus to his house) was really all about Simon's needs, not the needs of his guests.

As hosts we give our focus of attention to those who are our guests. Concerns about other matters are made secondary while we attend to the needs of our guests. Thoughtful availability directs our attention toward our guests and what we have that they need and we can offer them. Thoughtful availability places us in a servant mode, greatly valued in the model given to us by Jesus.

Reciprocity

We have already seen that host and guest share in vulnerability and humility, which become expressions of reciprocity. We take another step here in seeing the full participation of reciprocity in contexts of hospitality. Listening, we will see later, also is clearly reflective of reciprocity.

Abraham and Sarah participated in actions of hospitality aware of the potential reciprocity involved. The gift they received was so surprising that Sarah laughed at the possibility of the predicted birth—the absurdity that she could still give birth in her old age. Lot discovered that the hospitality he had shown to the strangers led to his and his family's rescue from death in the destruction of Sodom. The strangers became his family's means of survival in thwarting the intentions of the mob and in enabling them to escape from the imperiled city. These gifts were unexpected and surprisingly out of proportion to the hospitality that the hosts had offered. Even though our hosts, Abraham and Sarah and Lot and his family, *offered* their guests little, they, in truth, provided feasts for their visitors. Still, the gifts they received in return for their hospitality were "off the charts" of reciprocity.

The way-out-of-proportion nature of the gifts returned by those shown hospitality is evident in Jesus' encounter with the woman at Simon's house. Her gestures of hospitality toward Jesus, when Simon showed him none, were rewarded by the recognition of forgiveness of her sins, which Jesus identified as a result of her great love and by the assurance given to her by Jesus, "Your faith has saved you; go in peace" (Luke 7:50).

Hospitality has rewards, as we see in Matthew 25, in which Jesus reveals that the basis for reward from God looks a lot like offering hospitality. This passage is also important in introducing the concept that hospitality being offered to those in need is hospitality offered to Jesus. Those who offer the one who is thirsty a drink are offering a drink to Jesus, who assures them of their reward. Once again, the reward is far out of proportion to the original hospitality that was offered—a cup of water for your salvation.

The biblical characters that take the role of host are not doing so in order to receive a reward. There is no guarantee of a gift in return for hospitality. A reward is not their focus. Their motivation arises out of the strong traditional expectation/demand that hospitality be offered to those in need.

Hospitality involves a giving and receiving process. When we are given to generously, we must be able to *receive* generosity offered to us. When we are guests, we offer what we bring to the situation in which we are cast as the receivers. When we function as hosts, we give generously and must be open to receive what may come to us from our guest who originally came to us as one in need.

When we receive hospitality, we enter the situation as the ones in need, and yet we bring something the host needs. Some of us in the church, and especially in ministry, find it difficult to receive from others. Offering hospitality requires our willingness to receive from others *even as we are the ones in the position of offering hospitality*. We do not know what to expect, and may become uneasy at the prospect, and we still can feel assured that there will be *some* gift from the guest.

As guests we do not always know what we are going to bring to the host. This can feel uncomfortable for a guest who has not arrived with a traditionally identifiable hostess gift. What is more important in terms of reciprocity happens, though, in what takes place in the space of the visit, not so much in the offering of a box of candy that was brought for the host. The real gift from the guest is found in the relationship—in what transpires in their connection as host and guest.

For Abraham and Sarah, the gift was a renewal of the hope that God's promise to Abraham would indeed be fulfilled, in spite of the formidable barriers presented by the ages of the prospective parents. Hope was rekindled, even though Sarah laughingly responded to the announcement of their guests' prediction. The gift that is given is not the birth of a child, but the hope that lies in the promise revived.

Jesus' role as guest to Simon's invitation shifted to being guest to the caring woman who treated Jesus with the graciousness that Simon had neglected to demonstrate. In return, Jesus acknowledged to the woman what was already hers—both forgiveness and salvation. Abraham and Sarah's guests rekindle hope in what was already theirs (by God's promise). Within their interchanges as guests and hosts our biblical host-characters received invaluable gifts, which turn out (in two of the stories) to be reminders of what they already have.

The passage in Matthew 25:35-40 is joined by another in Hebrews to give us a further dimension of reciprocity.

> Do not neglect to show hospitality to strangers, for by doing that some have entertained angels without knowing it. Remember those who are in prison, *as though you were in prison* with them; those who are being tortured, *as though you yourselves were being tortured.* (Hebrews 13:2-3, emphasis mine)

In Matthew, Jesus said the familiar, "Truly I tell you, just as you did it to one of the least of these who are members of my family, you did it to me" (25:40). In these passages from Matthew and Hebrews we learn that we are to *see ourselves* as though we are in the place of those to whom we offer acts of hospitality—in the place of those in need, in other words. Being able to put ourselves in the shoes of another person is a part of hospitality that may be understood as reciprocity.

In the now-to-be-expected turnaround, those in need *are* Jesus. What we offer them, to meet their needs, is as though we offer it to Jesus. This passage also recalls the tradition of Abraham and Sarah and their guests in the desert, reinforcing the view that they offered generous hospitality unaware of the identity of those they served. My conclusion is that being Christian means being hospitable.

The Hebrews passage noted above points out that when we offer hospitality we do so with recognition that we put ourselves in the place of the one who is in need. When we offer, as hosts, we are to remember that we are also receiving in the place of the guest. The guest's struggle is our struggle. We identify with the person to whom we offer hospitality; we identify with the guest, the one who is in need, to whom we respond with our hospitality.

One woman offered a demonstration of reciprocity in hospitality during her terminal stay in the hospital. Shirley became the enthusiastic host of everyone who served her during her stay. Here she was the guest in terms of their care for her, but she persistently took on the role of being host to them. She insisted, even as she grew weaker, on having someone take her picture with each and every person who helped her or offered her service (and hospitality). Her camera was always nearby. When someone took her to X-ray, his or her picture was taken with her. When someone cleaned her room or changed her bed, their pictures were taken with her. Those who pushed her wheelchair from place to place were required to pose for their photo with her. Every visitor, every staff member; no one was left out. Every service person, no matter how small their task, went into her growing album. Shirley's actions reveal the back-and-forth, shifting between giving and receiving, alternating nature of hospitality that we are identifying as reciprocity in hospitality.

Shirley enthusiastically honored each person with whom she came into contact while she was in the hospital. I do not have a clearer image of someone keeping the faith. The roles of host and guest shifted regularly. Her ability to maintain reciprocity in her relationships with those upon whose service she was dependent was inspiring. The host on hand was clearly Jesus, as he was also the one who was represented in each person who served Shirley. Clearly she served Jesus in every person she honored. Those who served her also served Jesus.

Obedience in Hospitality

In addition to the qualities of hospitality that have been discussed and that we will be exploring in relation to the practice of listening in ministry, there is another further issue in relation to hospitality. Not only have we seen that hospitality is expected, but we also can see that hospitality is demanded/commanded. In order to be obedient followers of Jesus, we *must be* those who offer hospitality. In this section we will look at the issue of obedience in relation to hospitality. Might we also be *expected* to listen as part of our obedience to God?

In our examples from the Hebrew Scriptures, we see that our hosts were well aware of the requirement of both their faith and their culture to welcome strangers—to offer hospitality to those in need. Out of his commitment to what was expected by his faith, Lot insisted, against the resistance of the strangers, that they come to his home for the night rather than stay in the town square where they intended to remain (perhaps, from what the strangers had heard about Sodom, they had expected no one to offer them hospitality).[14] In the story about Jesus and the hospitable woman, the Pharisee, above all, should have been the one who was obedient; instead, the woman Simon viewed as unclean (as one who didn't keep the laws of the Torah) was the one who took up the command to offer hospitality.[15] The true host often emerges as an unexpected participant in the scene, as the one who is willing to be obedient. In the story of the Good Samaritan the surprising host turns out not to be the priest, and not the Levite, but the Samaritan, who was obedient and took on the role of being host to the robbed and beaten man.[16] The Samaritan's role as host did not end when he handed the wounded man over to another host, for he continued to provide what the man would need after he left him—he supplied another host to take over the role of host in his place and subsidized the new host.

First Peter 4:9 makes hospitality a direct order: "Be hospitable to one another without complaining." Within the list in which Paul defines the marks of the true Christian, along with "Love one another," "Rejoice in hope," and "Do not repay anyone evil for evil," we find "Extend hospitality to strangers" (Rom. 12:9-17). Who we are as Christians is hospitable. That is what is expected of us in doing the will of God under the guidance of Jesus Christ. We are those who extend hospitality to the stranger, welcome others, offer the needy what they lack, and give others space in our homes and hearts.

Interconnections of the Characteristics of Hospitality

Whereas I have gone to some lengths to understand hospitality by defining four different characteristics found in hospitality, these characteristics do not separate from one another neatly or clearly. We see that courage is necessary for both humility and vulnerability, and sometimes for thoughtful availability. Silence is an issue in thoughtful availability and in reciprocity, but also in humility. Conflict can bring all of the characteristics into play, calling on their presence to offer resolution.

Prayer, along with conflict, calls for the presence and interweaving of all four characteristics of hospitality. Humility, vulnerability, and thoughtful availability may be most evident in prayer, but I would challenge an understanding of prayer that excludes reciprocity. The characteristics of hospitality might be seen as a team working together as we proceed to see their application in listening.

Connecting Hospitality and Listening

In this chapter we have unpacked hospitality as it appears in several Scriptures. We see core qualities present in acts of hospitality: vulnerability, humility, thoughtful availability, and reciprocity. We also learn that in order to be obedient and faithful, we must become those who offer hospitality.

Hospitality requires that there be host and guest. At first sight we recognize who is the host and who are the guests, but we have discovered that the roles of host and guest may shift in the midst of a scene or as the scene comes to a close. We discover that this will also happen in acts of listening.

Hospitality involves the acts of welcoming and receiving, which are the essence of listening. When we indicate that we are willing to listen to someone, we have welcomed that person. When we listen and hear another person, we have received them. When we listen, we open ourselves not only to hear, but also to being vulnerable to our own pain as well as to the pain of the other. We recognize humility—having a right perspective on ourselves—which is required in order to be able to offer appropriate hospitality and effective listening.

What we experience and do in that process of welcoming and receiving in the practice of listening is the focus for the following chapters. We will in each of the next four chapters pick up one of the qualities of hospitality that have been presented and examine them as they can be brought to bear on our practice of listening.

Focus Questions

Recall a time when you experienced true hospitality.
What was the occasion?
Where were you?
Who provided the hospitality?
What was unexpected in the experience?
Can you name specific indicators that identified this experience as one of hospitality?
How did it feel to you to be the guest?

Exercise 1: Attentive Listening

Preparation: If you are using this book as a part of a class or any small group setting, this exercise is designed to take place during the first or second session within the context of the session/class. Participants should take the opportunity to introduce themselves to others, choosing to share something significant about themselves. This is not an opportunity for participants to tell where they are from or whether they are single or married. This is an opportunity to offer others something that is important to you, but may not be known by others. Offer something that feels comfortable to share. It is an opportunity to give others something to remember. Introductions should be random and not follow a course around the room from one side to the other. The leader should go first to model the exercise, but also to give participants some time to think. In this way, the leader also models hospitality. The leader should ask participants to share at will.

The Exercise: Now you are prepared. You no longer have to focus on yourself and what you are going to have to say. Put your introduction to the side until you are ready to present it and give the other participants your focus. The plan is for you to be able to fully attend to what the others are telling you about themselves. This is a challenge in listening. Your temptation will likely be to respond to what someone else says when you have heard a connection with your own life. "I came from Cincinnati, too. What school did you go to?"

The exercise is to practice *not* doing that. Listen as clearly as possible. Remember everyone's name. Feel free to ask for any clarifications you want from a speaker, not prolonging the exercise unduly. If you are comfortable with doing so and would find it helpful, make notes during the introductions. Notes can be about your own listening or to help you remember what others say and help you remember their names.

Follow-up: Make some notes to yourself about what you were doing as others spoke. When you lost focus on the speaker notice what led you away. Evaluate how well you are able to remain focused on the person speaking and do not be busy revising your own introduction. This is a good point for using a listening journal. Think about how you might work on anything you discovered that hindered your listening. What have you learned about your listening?

CHAPTER TWO

PREPARING TO LISTEN: HUMILITY IN LISTENING

Introduction

The greatest gift we bring to the listening process is ourselves. *And the most important thing to do in order to listen well is to keep ourselves out of the way.* Here we have a fundamental paradox in listening. We bring to the task of listening our lives of experiences—what we have learned in relationships with family and friends, in church and community, in classes and supervision for ministry, in clinical pastoral education, and in ministry experiences. *Something* in all of this will help us understand what someone says to us, but *any of this also has the potential for blocking what we are able to hear.*

Human experience draws us, as we listen to another, to "filling in" from our own lives, in which case we *tend not to hear* the person to whom we are "listening." Our own experience takes the focus and abandons its potential for being a *gift for listening* and becomes instead a *barrier to listening.* Self-awareness enables us to recognize when we are getting in the way of the listening we are trying to do—when we have added our own experience to the speaker's story.

In order to listen accurately to another person we need unflinching, compassionate, and bold self-awareness. We only achieve self-awareness when we are able to see ourselves with appropriate humility. Effective listening emerges in a context of appropriate humility and honest self-awareness.

The paradox is always present: we have to keep our selves out of the way, and our selves are our best gifts to effective listening.

Primary in preparation for listening is self-awareness. Self-awareness, rigorously applied, helps spare us from listening disasters. I would even propose that lack of, or seriously limited self-awareness makes *effective* listening impossible—not improbable—but truly impossible. In this chapter we will examine the many ways in which we need to be sharply self-aware and the potential disasters that may result from failures in self-awareness. We also will see illustrations of self-awareness at work to the benefit of listening.

This chapter explores many of the circumstances that get in the way of our listening and introduces how honest self-awareness provides a foundation for enabling us to listen effectively in the midst of all that would interfere with what we hear.

Underlying our ability to attain self-awareness is the need for the functioning of an appropriate measure of humility. In chapter 1 we examined humility as a quality of hospitality. Here we will look at the practice of humility in developing and maintaining self-awareness essential to effective listening. We begin with an examination of how we can claim a new understanding of humility—an understanding that we began to approach in chapter 1.

Humility as Perspective

Understanding humility as a proper perspective on oneself may feel like a contradiction to the way you have understood humility. I used to shudder at the mention of humility or the suggestion of being humble because I heard it as indicative of groveling, diminishing oneself, becoming a doormat for others. A diminished self is not what humility is about.

Let us return briefly to the scene at Simon the Pharisee's house, where we see the courageous woman washing Jesus' feet with her tears, drying them with her hair, and putting ointment on his feet. I used to see this as an act that was very servile (in keeping with my former view of humility), but a deeper understanding of the scripture (as suggested in chapter 1) and a look at the whole situation changes that picture. Her acts of offering Jesus hospitality were not only providing honor to a guest—honor that Simon, as host, neglected to provide—but were also in-your-face actions in relation to Simon as the identified host of the event.

The woman had an accurate perspective on herself that was rooted in appropriate humility. She knew what she had to offer and knew what should be done according to cultural tradition and religious expectations. Lacking water, she used her tears. Lacking a towel, she used her hair. She stepped into the role of functioning as host to Jesus to undo the insult from Simon who failed to provide for Jesus the appropriate rituals of hospitality. Honest humility enables us to have more accurate perspectives of others as well as ourselves. This woman, scorned by the Pharisees, could see the Pharisees—even the "host" of the household—as challengeable.

Simon, in contrast, seems to have thought much more highly of himself than was appropriate. His focus was on himself, and his self-assessment was inflated. He probably insulted Jesus because he was threatened by Jesus' teachings. At the same time, he held his own higher position as Pharisee as more honorable than Jesus' position. Simon wanted to "show Jesus up," but the guest-turned-host woman turned the tables on him. Looking at this woman and Simon we see a contrast between his pride and her humility.

Pride may be seen as the opposite to humility—as an expression of arrogance. I find neither concept—pride or humility—helpful, *as they have been traditionally understood* (nor do I find it helpful to see them as opposites). Some degree of pride is quite appropriate—even for Christians. To have appropriate pride means to have self-esteem and self-respect, to recognize oneself as a person with particular gifts who is a child of God, deeply loved by God.

To have excessive pride means being arrogant and haughty, imagining oneself as "all that" (some would add, "and a bag of chips") and basically flawless. Pride is understood as an exaggerated sense of self-esteem. The absence of pride means degradation, inhuman diminishing of oneself. I now find it helpful to think of humility more appropriately as a right perspective on oneself. With such a right perspective one attains a balance between one's level of pride and one's level of humility, both of which are appropriate. Appropriate levels of pride and humility assure us that we are neither everything nor are we nothing.

We do not have to be caught in this polarized sense of being human that pushes us to one extreme, of pride, or the other, of humility, rather than encouraging clear, realistic, honest self-assessment. An honest self-assessment will lead us to recognize the gifts we have and the limitations within which we function. Accurate and compassionate self-assessment is difficult and requires honest self-awareness. Honest self-awareness usually finds us more in balance— recognizing what we do have and what we don't. Humility is at the heart of this balance. Christian community is nourished in this balance, as a place where giving and receiving are honored.

The humility shown by Abraham, Sarah, and Lot when they offered strangers a bit of bread, a little water, and a brief rest diminished what they really were able to and were going to offer. They avoided saying to their guests that they would "go all out" to entertain them (even in order to entice them out of their reluctance to accept the offer of hospitality) out of a polite sense that minimized the hard work and the demand on available resources that would be necessary to entertain their guests. It was not a denial of what they had to offer, but a way of inviting guests that would not make them uncomfortable by being made aware of the extent to which the host had to go to entertain them properly.

In our role of listening to another we can convey this sense of appropriate humility and self-awareness, or we can convey that we will have whatever the guest needs and all we have to do is listen to them and we will help. When we act as though we can give the speaker answers and *make* them feel better, communicating that we are able to fix everything or solve their problems, we betray humility and the effective practice of listening.

We enter the listening event with recognition that we may have what the speaker can use because we are ready to welcome and receive the speaker and allow the speaker to determine where we go in the conversation. Our humility and self-awareness also provide awareness that we may not have what is needed. We know what we have to offer, and we know where our limitations are. We are open to hear what the speaker brings. Since it is so rare, the very act of welcoming and receiving what the speaker has to say is itself healing.

Being Honest with Ourselves

Appropriate self-awareness requires that we be honest with ourselves. Yet, many of us have significant trouble being honest with ourselves. Maybe we don't trust ourselves. Maybe we fear seeing ourselves as we truly are. How can this be when, as Christians, we affirm that we are created by God and remain part of God's family, God's own precious, beloved children?

Part of the answer to that question rests in messages we receive, and have received for as long as we have lived. Many messages from the people and the world around us (including people who love us and communities that embrace us) give us information for how we evaluate ourselves.

These messages do not have to be congruent with reality. In the face of all of the messages we receive, we cannot but lack honest self-awareness.

The church has played an important role in influencing our perceptions of ourselves. We have been told that we are sinners. We have been told not to be proud, and therefore have learned to diminish ourselves. We have been told to be humble, and therefore have, well, diminished ourselves. We absorb so much that defies any view of ourselves as gifted, treasured, and beloved by God, that being honest with ourselves may be something we would rather avoid.

Some others hold an equally low self-assessment, but act as though they surely are the best and the greatest. They have a bad case of over-esteem for themselves. Their behavior belies their true feelings. These people have just as hard a time honestly looking at themselves. The ministry has its share of these people, just as it has its share of those who underesteem themselves.

Honestly looking at ourselves, with appropriate humility, turns out to be an act of courage and holds the potential for abundant blessings. When we do not accurately assess ourselves we end up closed off to some of the blessings we might receive. Thinking we are "all that," we see no need to receive from others. Thinking that we are nothing, we find ourselves unworthy to receive from others. Honest self-assessment and accurate humility are more likely to allow us to receive blessings from others and form a strong basis for community.

The existence of human community is rooted in the reality that each of us needs others, because none of us has all that we need to survive. We all bring something to the human table that some others at the table need. None of us has all we need and none of us has nothing to bring. Such a recognition allows us to enter into listening with expectations that we will both give what the speaker needs and receive something we need.

Self-Awareness in Listening

Listening well requires that we have awareness of our attitudes in matters of race, class, gender, culture, age, religion, language, sexual orientation, level of education, marital status, disabilities, gender roles, political affiliation, and so on. *All of us* have some prejudices and stereotypes. We have views that have not yet been challenged in our lives. We hold views that we assume and have not taken opportunities to question. We actively function out of some views and attitudes that perhaps we are not even aware that we have. In addition to the categories of differences named above, most, if not all of us, come with life-inflicted wounds that may carry the power to bias our thinking.

Back at Simon's house again: At the end of Jesus' dialogue with Simon, Jesus said to Simon, "Therefore, I tell you, her many sins are forgiven because she loved much."[1] Jesus then said to the woman, "Your sins are forgiven" (Luke 7:48). What the others at the table *heard Jesus say* was that *he* forgave her sins. They responded, "Who is this who even forgives sins?" Their question could be reworded, "Who does he think he is?" Their view of Jesus—what they expected from him—caused them to not hear him accurately. Jesus did not claim to forgive her sins. Rather, what Jesus said pointed to and affirmed the action of God.[2]

This brief glimpse into scripture demonstrates how we can mishear someone. We bring to the moment when someone speaks, our past experience of that person, in particular. Sometimes we bring misconceptions we have about this particular person or others like them, anticipating what they might do and *what we expect to hear and see from them*, which can prevent us from clearly hearing what they say or seeing what they do.

Underlying the hearing of the Pharisees gathered at the table was an urge to find fault with Jesus. He was stirring up too much trouble with his unorthodox interpretation of the Torah, with which they were at odds. They, along with Simon, were eager to discredit him. We operate in ways very similar to the Pharisees in this biblical scene when we listen *without* honest self-awareness, holding our views in absolute certainty, bearing attitudes and expectations that cannot be overcome by what the person we are hearing actually says. Humility is not in the house.

We understand some of our views to be biblically supported. In these cases it does not seem like we hold prejudices, but rather have a view that is *right* according to our faith. In this we might resemble Simon and the Pharisees. They held certain interpretations of the Torah that Jesus challenged. To them, he was not being faithful. Because his interpretations differed from theirs, they had some difficulty listening to him, and misheard what he said.

Our aim must be to know whatever will become barriers to our listening and hearing well, and be able to attend to these barrier-causes. Some of our barriers involve conviction that we are absolutely right in our understanding of certain theological views that others see differently.

When this is where we find ourselves, we can deal with the barriers by remaining open to growth in faith and understanding, assured that the Holy Spirit is not done with us yet. This stance only comes from appropriate humility and accurate self-awareness, grounded in a deep faith.

Listening is impeded when we hold theological views so tightly that to hear a different view is threatening. Our ability to welcome, receive, and hear another is threatened when we sense they may hold views that differ from our own. We may find ourselves holding onto the control of the conversation, directing it to other areas or tuning out so that we do not hear. This is a way to avoid conflict in our listening role.

We bring to every moment of listening attitudes, prejudices, unhealed wounds, impressions, and expectations that may or may not be related to that particular person and situation and may have more to do with our experiences with others or even our feelings about ourselves. What we bring from outside to the present situation—to this particular listening moment—interferes with what we hear when we come to the moment, *unless* we are able to come to the moment with consistent and honest self-awareness.

We can come to the listening moment with particular attitudes, presuppositions, and expectations and, through self-awareness, be able to recognize them for what they are. One woman described her experience of talking with her pastor. He was new to the church and they had not had a private conversation before. He began the conversation by checking out his assumptions with her. He discovered that what he had presumed was not true and their conversation continued on a different basis.

First, the pastor needed the self-awareness that allowed him to recognize that he had assumptions about the parishioner. Then he was able to find out if they were correct or not and clear away whatever misconceptions he had. His awareness cleared the way for his listening to be more effective.

Self-Awareness in Action:
A Learning Experience

In the class I teach, which is an introduction to pastoral care, I ask students to find a partner and schedule time to meet and take turns listening to each other. Each partner has one period of time to be the speaker and another to be the listener. At the heart of the assignment is the opportunity to evaluate one's listening in a safe environment. In the process, the partner to whom they have listened also evaluates each student. (For more details on this exercise and complete instructions for doing it, see Exercise 2 at the end of this chapter.)

One man wrote his self-evaluation with more honesty and humility than I had seen in any other self-evaluating paper. He boldly confessed that he was only able to listen to his partner for a very brief time before he was compelled to take over the speaking. From that point on, the partner who was supposed to be speaking did not get much, if any, chance to speak.

I think I gave him an A on the assignment. He listened poorly—probably the worst in the class, and he wonderfully demonstrated his ability to be honestly self-aware. In his paper, he wrote about how he understood his inability/unwillingness to listen to his partner. *This* was the whole point of the assignment. He got it! He paid attention to himself *as* he was trying to listen to his partner. He recognized that he abandoned the assignment when he took over and kept the speaking role. He made no excuses for what he had done. He demonstrated appropriate humility in being able to come clean in his paper and clearly admit that in the activity he had failed to do what he was supposed to do. Excessive pride or traditional humility could have prevented him from his honest revelations about his functioning in listening. His learning from the experience would have stopped right there.

His job, following this experience, became trying to understand what it was that compelled him to talk and, consequently, to avoid listening to his partner. From that point he could work on what he needed to do in the future in order to become a better listener. I doubt that his work was completed without doing and reflecting on this assignment. I imagine that it took more reflection and experience to work to a new place where he would be able to listen effectively.

This student was exemplary in self-awareness. The way he used this exercise gave him a starting point. Other students, who were kind to themselves or to their listening partners and proposed only mild critiques of themselves or their partners, may have missed the value of the gift to be found in deeper self-awareness and the humility to expose the truth about the listening they did without making excuses.

Self-Awareness and Limitations

Preparing to listen requires, within our self-awareness, knowledge of where our limits lie. I have deeply appreciated a few students in my teaching experience who have voluntarily informed me that they have been diagnosed with ADD (Attention Deficit Disorder) or ADHD (Attention Deficit Hyperactive Disorder). Informing a professor that one has such a disorder could be terribly embarrassing. Yet these students told me and proceeded to inform me of how their diagnosed disorder affected their behavior in particular.

In every instance, they told me that they might have to get up during class to walk around or leave the room. Another mentioned his tendency to fidget, wanting me to understand the cause of his actions. Their knowledge of themselves indicated in their self-descriptions is important knowledge for their ministries.

Once one is aware that something will affect one's actions and behavior and how it will do so, then one is free to seek ways in which ministry needs to be shaped in order to allow for one's limitations. This kind of limitation may mean that the pastor might schedule meetings or visits in such a way that allow the freedom to move around as needed. My point is that when we are honest with ourselves and others around us (as this is necessary) we are enabled to function more effectively within personal contexts that would otherwise feel limiting and that would, therefore, function as limitations.

ADD and ADHD usually mean limitations for listening. Self-awareness and appropriate humility allow pastors with struggles or problems like these to recognize how their conditions might become barriers to listening and to find ways to reduce the influence of their conditions on their listening. Awareness of any barriers to listening makes it possible for pastor/listeners to find ways to compensate for what could limit their listening.

Self-Awareness to the Rescue

A number of years ago, while I was leading a workshop for pastors, I met an important ally. I had been leading the group of about a dozen pastors, and had done a lot of talking for most of a day, when suddenly one of the participants jumped up and shouted at me, "I don't agree with a thing you have said yet!"[3]

This was when I discovered what I call "my great internal NO!" What the pastor said felt devastating, and I recognized immediately that I was facing strong defensive feelings and potential conflict. Visually, I see the gesture of my hands stretched out in front of me, palms facing my "attacker," ready to fend off what is said—as if something had been thrown at me. This signals for me a refusal to listen. The gesture signals defense. My concern is focused on protecting myself and not on understanding the speaker.

Somehow—and this is where I affirm the working of the Holy Spirit—out of nowhere I was inspired to ask the pastor, "Tell me just what you haven't agreed with." I remember my voice being calm. I remember that I didn't jump to my feet to defend myself against this attack. I did not write off this pastor as the only one who "wasn't getting it." I didn't assume that he was just a complainer and give his outburst a moment of acknowledgment; nor did I simply say, "Sorry about that," and then move along. I also remember that I had no idea where my response came from and only later did I name it as the work of the Holy Spirit (and remain convinced of that source to this day). I don't want to underestimate the difficulty of being able to respond in this way. It surely takes the power of the Holy Spirit to be able to do it.

As the conversation continued, the pastor listed a few things with which he disagreed and I clarified points that he had misunderstood. Then we arrived at one point on which it was clear that we did not agree. The session ended not too long after our encounter, and the pastor who had "attacked" me hurried to speak to me to voice his appreciation for my response.

The pastor had not really attacked me, but my great internal NO! defiantly told me he did. The gift of the moment for me was that I discovered that my great internal NO! was not the boss of me. I could acknowledge its warning, turn down its volume, gently put it to the side, and allow myself to listen and hear. I effectively lowered my defenses. My hands moved from their protective position (remember, this is all done mentally, but could be done physically to give emphasis to the shift in response) to a gesture of receptivity—palms outstretched, open, facing up to receive.

What my great internal NO! signaled for me was a threat. Its response came in a defensive mode out of a place of fear. I discovered I didn't have to stay there. I could respond from another part of me and be open to a saving inspiration, surprisingly made available to me, as a gift.

I have since suspected that everyone has their very own great internal NO! Our work is to recognize it (self-awareness), turn down its volume, and step aside (humility), not giving it free rein; for when we do, it is then that it will launch us into a full-scale conflict where there need not be one. Sometimes I am not able to function in the way I have described and recommended. My response is not always open and my NO! can take over. Even at those times I am glad I remember that it does not always have to be so. I remember my Holy Spirit ally and anticipate doing better the next time. When I am able to respond with this kind of openness it is compassionate self-awareness and humility at work under the guidance of the Holy Spirit.

Barriers to Listening Well

Every one of us has some issues that we would prefer to avoid. I have seen in ministry that when there is something you want to avoid, count on it showing up and presenting itself for your ministry. If I want to listen well, I must know what I want or need to avoid and be able to recognize the signs of my avoidance. Sometimes these are the same areas in which I have prejudicial feelings. Otherwise, feelings of not wanting to deal with particular issues come from my life experiences in which something may have so influenced my life that I cannot face it in the life of another person.

It is possible that I could heal this part of my past and then be able to offer myself as a listener to someone with a related struggle, but that is not possible to do *at the moment* when I face someone in need. Such pain-filled barriers may catch us by surprise. When I cannot deal with something and heal around it, compassionate, bold self-awareness is the gift I need. I must know what I cannot go near—what I have to avoid. Discovering what these things are is best done before they meet us in a person who comes to us in need.

Many years ago in a class on human sexuality that I taught, a student took on the role of a person who had been raped.[4] After some struggle, she admitted to me that every time she began to read on the topic she started to cry. She didn't understand why this was happening, but since she was a conscientious student, it was very troubling to her. An experience like hers should always be a signal that there is something waiting to be understood, discovered, and healed. Finally she recalled, for the first time in her life, that she had been sexually abused as a child.

Facing the topic of rape, although the scenario was not exactly what she had experienced, was too closely related to her experience and brought out long-forgotten feelings related to it.[5] Feelings that had been repressed and that she had kept hidden from herself flew into her awareness. In the end she bravely made her way through the assignment (that also included writing a paper about the role experience), doing well. Through this experience she moved toward becoming better equipped to be able to receive and listen to someone who had been raped or sexually abused.

Experiences like this student's are better had within an educational or therapeutic setting rather than during a listening experience in which one is in a ministerial, caring role. The woman in this story could have found herself subconsciously avoiding allowing anyone who had been raped or sexually abused to speak to her on these issues. Her own recognition—deep down—could have put up barriers to hearing and could have been a barrier that prevented another person's healing in her care. If such painful issues had been brought up by someone in her care she might have found herself unable to listen with effectiveness. Her focus would have turned toward herself and she would still have had to figure out why.

If listeners meet this kind of barrier in their practice of pastoral listening, what they communicate to the speaker may be very painful. Experiences of sexual abuse and rape are very wounding and frequently kept secret from others and even from oneself. To be able to bring such an experience and the feelings related to it into a pastoral conversation often takes great courage. To have this moment of courage met with the listener's unself-aware fears—fears that may have kept the abused from bringing the experience to light sooner—may feel like rejection and judgment to the speaker. The experience could reinforce the shame already present for the speaker.

Another arena of avoidance is related to fears I have. *We all have fears.* Having points of fear is not cause for judgment. Any judgment is related only to willingness to be aware of myself and act in a way that will protect those who are in my care from being hurt or neglected because of my fears. Fears and the things I want to avoid are not clearly divided from each other. Some of my fears may be related to things I want to avoid, others may not.

Pastors cannot aspire realistically to be persons with no fears and no prejudices, but we can hold ourselves accountable to an unrelenting practice of self-awareness. The willingness to see myself honestly and wholly demands humility and courage to come face-to-face with my own scary stuff. When I cannot look at my own shadowy self, my negative and painful experiences, I will hang back from listening to the shadowy and negative stuff that others bring to me (or I fear they could bring to me) seeking healing.

When someone begins to go into places I have feared to go myself, I will have to shut them down. I will not be able to take the risk of allowing them to go there, let alone the risk of going with them. I might do this by giving them a quick answer to a complex problem. I might change the subject, redirecting the conversation to avoid a threatening or scary subject. I may simply suggest that we pray about it before the conversation has gone too far for my comfort level.

Some areas are neither fears nor prejudices that I have, nor are they related to my shadow self, but may simply be places where I just do not want to go. Generally, these places involve some strong feelings—shame, guilt, fear, rage, grief. One woman, a longtime church member and well loved in her congregation, reflected that whenever she brought up the subject of her mother (who was recently deceased) to anyone in the church, they would change the subject. One reason for this could be the desire of those with whom she spoke to help her avoid "feeling bad." The reaction she received is very common among church people in relation, especially, to feelings of grief. Divorce, miscarriage, loss of a job, or a death in the family may be met with an early expression of condolence, but thereafter avoided.

Talking or not talking about a person one grieves does not determine whether one feels the pain of the loss or not. This is true even when talking may bring a new flow of tears. Regardless, the pain was *already there*. Conversation, an invitation to talk about the loss, and an openness to allow the pain and tears to come into one's presence as a listener, provides another step toward healing through the grief process.

Avoidance of and failure to listen carefully to someone's grief also may signal our own unfinished grief from some loss that could be many years old. The pain and sadness of another can touch our own pain and sadness. We recall our experiences filled with pain. As the pastor/listener, we may shy away from persons' expressions of strong feelings because we do not want to feel our own strong feelings or let others know we have these feelings.

Areas of life that are heavily laden with feelings—sexuality, death, aging, race—will be difficult areas for listening. So many strong emotions are attached to these issues that they are difficult subjects for us to hear effectively. As pastors, these issues are easily among the top issues for parishioners of all ages. Somehow every pastor must recognize any discomfort in these areas and work toward greater comfort. Reading for information and understanding can make a very important contribution to greater ability to listen. Exposure to the areas that we find difficult will help our listening. But gaining information is not the whole answer; because these issues are so emotional and so personal, honest self-awareness is absolutely essential.

Conflict and Criticism in Listening

Conflict (or any *threat* of conflict) and criticism seriously limit our ability to listen. Most of us in ministry fear and avoid both. My experience with the outspoken pastor in that workshop included possibilities of both conflict and criticism. When either conflict or criticism cause us to stop or limit our listening—signaled by feelings of needing to defend ourselves—we need a reliable, functioning, appropriate humility. Conflicts and criticism escalate in the presence of defensiveness and are deflated with an accurate sense of oneself as both gifted and flawed. What is this person saying that may be useful to me? or Where is this comment coming from? could be questions to remember when we feel defense bubbling up.[6]

Conflict with or between individuals or within a congregation is the time most needing excellence in listening. Especially in times of conflict, the character of humility and its support for accurate self-assessment are necessary. Conflicts create an astonishing inability to hear one another. Conflict taps into our defensiveness, which inhibits our openness to receiving the other. Churches frequently get into conflicts. Some churches perpetually maintain conflict.

All of the same can be said of criticism. Criticism creates the defensiveness we may associate with conflict, which means further challenge to listening well. Pastors can be targets of criticism at times and struggle with what they would do well to hear, even when the criticism seems unjustified. Being able to be effectively, compassionately, and honestly self-aware enables pastors to evaluate criticism as it comes our way.

Control in Listening

For many of us resistance to fully listening comes in the realization that fully listening to another means that we have to let go of control of the situation. It is impossible for a listener to keep control of the conversation and also allow someone to speak freely. As listeners we do not know where speakers will take us—unless we are in control of the conversation. When we remain in control, we are less likely to run into any of our fears, prejudices, or uncomfortable areas.

Our urge to keep asking a speaker questions is one way we are assured of keeping ourselves in control of what is going to come out in the conversation. One pastor turned the direction of a woman's speaking about her battering husband by asking her, "Do you still love your husband?"[7] What he was saying to her was, "Let's talk instead about the loving side of your relationship." (Subtext: I can't deal with the violence/conflict.) An alternative many pastors have used is, "What did you do to make him hit you?" turning the blame and the shame on the woman and again avoiding the violence of the husband.

Deeply listening to another person creates intimacy between the speaker and the listener. When we want to avoid intimacy with others or with particular others (those whom I find to be too attractive or repulsive to me) we will avoid effective listening. The avoidance of deep listening helps us maintain control over the situation, the relationship, and ourselves. What we also avoid is the experience of being host to someone who may be in need of being heard. Intimacy does not have to mean sexuality or sexual behavior. Self-awareness is our best aid in maintaining listening intimacy without moving to sexual intimacy.

When Connections Betray: Talking with Marge

In the pastoral role, being able to hear from people in their struggles, literally with *any* human experience, challenges the pastor's imagination. There are some things I may never understand! How then can I play a helping role with a parishioner whose experience is far removed from my own?

I was fresh out of seminary, in my first ministry position. I was working with the youth of the church and with the education program. The mother of one of the boys from the youth group came to talk with me about her son. Even though Joe came to youth meetings regularly, he remained a peripheral member of the group. I did not experience any trouble with him in the youth group. Marge, Joe's mother, was struggling with some problems with him at home. From the beginning of her description of what was going on, it sounded familiar to me. The connection I felt was from my own family. Joe's behavior reminded me of my brother as a teenager.[8] I blurted out, "He's just like my brother!"

Marge's face brightened up. I could see hope radiating from her smile as she eagerly asked, "How did he turn out?" Whoops! At that time my brother was going through some difficult times. What was I going to say to her? I have no idea what I said, but surely it couldn't have been very authentic.

The struggle is between allowing what I know from my experience to *help me hear*, but not let it *determine what I hear*. What is the difference between these two possibilities? On one hand, I am reading into the situation by reading out of the narrative of my own experience. On the other hand, I am allowing my experience to play in the background, at a low volume, while I listen for differences that exist between my experiences and the experiences the speaker describes to me. Once I saw the connection between Joe and my brother, I wanted to let Marge know that I really understood. My attempt at demonstrating that I had made a connection with what she was saying clearly backfired.

In this instance I was not operating out of an appropriate level of humility. I wanted badly to meet Marge's expectations that I could help with her son, but I was distracted from what I might have been able to offer her by my own feelings of insecurity and a lack of self-awareness, which led me into trouble. Yes, my experience with my brother might have been helpful in understanding Joe, but it had no place in our conversation. Its role was in my private reflections and not in my words to Marge. In other words, connections in your own life with what has been said may be a help to you, but are not likely to help the speaker.

In my experience with Marge another factor was operating that led me to respond inappropriately. I liked and respected Marge. As the minister working with the youth, and still young myself, I experienced my position as being somewhat caught between youth and adulthood. I wanted very much to make a connection with Marge that might be more of a friend-to-friend connection than a minister-to-parishioner connection. If I could do that, I could then see myself as being beyond that caught-between, neither-here-nor-there place between youth and adulthood. I could establish a friendship with a woman I respected and liked.

But these intentions were all focused on me and not on listening to Marge. My response had the effect of diminishing what Marge had said.

What I was looking for would violate the relationship we had. Establishing a friendship was not possible, and I had to recognize the loss of that possibility. I suspect that wanting a friendship-relationship may be a common motivation for responses in which the listener draws connections with the speaker, as I did.

Other moments of recognizing a connection with what someone is describing draw us into saying things such as, "I know just what you're feeling," or "I had the same experience." Not true. You do *not* know exactly how someone else feels and you have *not* had the same experience. When we hear connections that lead us to these thoughts, our work is just beginning. At that point, what I have to do is work harder at discovering what the difference is. The closer the experience seems to mine, the harder I must work to find the differences—so that I am hearing their experience and not my own story.

Whenever I see another person as being like me, I must work hard to hear the differences between who we are and our experiences. The temptation to see the similarities and go no further (because now I understand) is very strong. This temptation can provide a signal for us to become aware of how we are different. If I am going to listen effectively, I have to give our differences consistently focused attention.

When I listen to someone who is obviously different from me, I already know I have to work at understanding how the differences shape what is being said and what has been experienced.

Recoveries in Listening

With Marge, I recognize that I did not do a good job. I don't remember ever going back to talk with her about how I had failed her. I needed to grow into more humility and self-awareness before I could think about what I now speak of as recovering. Recoveries in listening are times when I recognize I was not listening to or misheard a speaker and I choose to return to the scene of the crime and admit my shortcoming. All is not lost when I can return and attempt to recover the situation. I believe that it is never too late. Recovery is a gracious, hospitable move.

Every conversation deserves a postreflective time in which the listener reviews what took place and evaluates his or her listening and the responses that were given. At times, awareness strikes when I am in the midst of listening. I realize I have missed something important or made a poor response. In either case, sooner or later, humility and self-awareness lead me to recall the moment with the speaker and try to recover what I missed.

Recovery during the conversation could go something like this: "I want us to back up a bit. You said something that seems like it could be important. I noticed it, but I failed to make any response. (Or, "Its significance didn't hit me until we had passed it by.") Could we return to the point at which you said. . . ?"

To illustrate follow-up after a conversation was over: Pastor Ruth reflects her conversation with parishioner Sue. Ruth realizes that Sue made a passing reference to a painful childhood experience and then just went on to other matters she was discussing. Ruth had let it pass, but in her postreflective time that moment stuck out like a sore thumb. Ruth wondered why she had let it go by and now felt she would need to go back to see Sue again to discover what she had so briefly referred to. Ruth is aware that it could be something in her own experience that prevented her from truly hearing Sue at that time.

Ruth will go back and she will tell Sue that she had been thinking about their conversation and recalled what she heard Sue say. After Ruth checks with Sue regarding what she heard Sue say, Pastor Ruth will indicate that it seemed like it could be something important and invite Sue to return to that moment (which I see as an instance of a door being opened just a crack, and then closed, or left open and walked away from).

Sue will have the choice to return with Pastor Ruth and open the door further to let Ruth in, or she will choose not to go there. Sue might even correct the pastor's understanding of what took place and demonstrate how Pastor Ruth misunderstood her. This could reflect that Ruth did not hear accurately, or it could be Sue's decision to continue to avoid whatever the issue might be.

Significant communication has taken place even when Sue decides not to talk about whatever it was to which she alluded. What has been accomplished is that Sue now knows that she can talk about whatever it is with her pastor. Her trust for her pastor, far from being weakened by finding out that Ruth is human, will be enhanced by this experience. Her own self-esteem will be raised—"The pastor values me enough to go away and think about our conversation when she has so much else to do." And, "It looks like I could talk about [that issue] with Pastor Ruth, after all. Maybe the next time we talk, I will be able to follow through on it." Humility is written all over this experience.

Humility in Listening Action

As humility determined that Abraham and Lot would downplay what they would provide to their guests, the listener is in the position of being aware that we do not and cannot simply fix the deep struggles and pains of our guests/parishioners. There are ways we can approach the task of listening that convey to the speaker that we are prepared to give them the answers and heal all of their wounds. Or we can offer a stance that simply says we are ready to receive and can be trusted with whatever is spoken.

Humility is not functioning when I feel compelled to fix it, make it better, or give the right answer. These goals in listening have nothing to do with humility. When we tell someone, "I know exactly what you are going through"; "That is just like what happened to me"; or "I know how you feel," we are experiencing a failure of humility and a breakdown in listening. None of these come out of effective listening. Our compulsions to do something deny the reality that the speaker has the need to tell the story—talking out the pain more than finding a solution "out there" somewhere. Many times we discover effective listening has the power to enable the speaker to discover the answer inside themselves.

Hospitality and the humility in hospitality recognize that the one who speaks to me, to whom I am listening, is on a journey. Our stay with each other will be brief in this moment when I am offering you hospitality. I remember that I will not have everything you will need, and it is not necessary that I do. I am acting in service to you as I welcome your speaking, and receive your words, and attend to your discovery of your answers.

Preparing to Listen in the Future

Some of the issues that parishioners will bring to us are way out of the range of our experience—matters with which we have no connection. The life experience of the other gender, although I live and work in the midst of people of the other gender, may still be a mystery to me. Drug addicts, homeless persons, prostitutes, and purveyors of pornography may be far from my experience. We only learn about some things by being exposed to the different culture in which these others, unknown by me, live their lives.

Preparing to Listen in the Moment

I prepare for each time of listening that I anticipate. As I approach a hospital visit I think through the circumstances of the person who is hospitalized. How much do I know about the reason for the hospitalization? How important is what I know/don't know? I think about this and put it aside. Concern with what is wrong with the patient should not be my focus when I enter the hospital room. I think about the family and friends involved, and other church members who are touched by the life of the patient. I think about the faith journey of the person to the extent that I am familiar with it. What is the state of our relationship? What is the importance of the person to the church? What are my feelings about hospitals? Illness? Doctors?

I take time to identify to myself and set aside those matters or issues that currently clutter my personal and ministerial horizon. What if this visit is to an elderly person and I am currently struggling with the care of my own aged parent? If I give all of these matters my attention before I go into the hospital room, and thoughtfully and prayerfully set them aside before I enter the door, they will have less power to hinder my listening.

Perhaps this process sounds like adding more clutter to what is already demanding my attention. My preparations to listen have to allow enough time for a process of clearing and letting go. I cannot begin to prepare *just outside of the patient's door*. When I enter the room, my goal is to focus on the patient/parishioner so I acknowledge all of these potential interferences in order to set them all aside and remove them from my focus.

One doctor tells how she imagines all of her baggage that she carries with her around the hospital as being in a large sack. As she stops outside a patient's room, before she enters, she imagines dropping the sack. She will be ready to pick it up again when she leaves the room. It will be there waiting for her. It is not going to go anywhere while she gives her focus to the patient she is visiting. She knows that this baggage has no place in her patient's room.

What this example describes is a process of clearing space in oneself so that there will be room to welcome, receive, and yes, entertain the patient/parishioner. This process necessitates radical self-awareness. I also prepare by allowing time to pray before entering the room. Prayer facilitates my setting aside all that would crowd into the room with me to distract my attention and prevent the patient from feeling welcome and received (instances when I have no space to offer). Prayer also reassures me that I bring to the room some important gifts that I may be able to offer the patient and reminds me that I do not enter the room alone. Prayer is a way of preparing myself to welcome and receive the person I visit. Prayer with the patient as we begin a visit enables both of us to enter into a sacred encounter of speaking and listening.

With prayer and an awareness of hospitality as it has been discussed thus far, I also enter the hospital room with expectations. The roles of host and guest are both shared by the pastor and the patient. I am approaching and entering the room that is the room of the patient, so I am the patient's guest. As the guest I will receive hospitality from the patient. The patient is also my guest since I enter the room to offer service to the patient. I also welcome the patient into the space I bring with me. There, I am the host.

Conclusion

Effective listening requires honest self-awareness grounded in appropriate humility. Being self-aware helps us recognize our limitations in listening. Humility is crucial to effective listening when it enables us to recognize our failures in listening and those things that threaten to bring us to listening failures. Humility helps us prepare for listening and recover from listening shortcomings. The humility demonstrated in the hospitality shown by Abraham, Sarah, Lot, and the gracious woman at Simon's house are models for our listening intents.

Focus Questions

What hinders your honest self-awareness?

What issues do you expect could be brought to you in your practice of ministry that you clearly do not want to deal with?

What do these issues mean to you? Where do they connect with your life/experience?

If you see no connection, how do you understand these issues as becoming avoidance issues for you?

Exercise 2: Partners in Listening

Introduction: In this exercise, you will need a partner. In a class, your partner should be another class member. Each of you will function as speaker one time, and at another time as listener. Both roles are important to the exercise. The focus of the exercise is to *evaluate your own listening*. What is said by the speaker is merely a vehicle to your assessment as the listener. In this exercise you also get the help of the speaker to assess your listening. In ordinary life and in ministry we do not have the opportunity to get help in intentional feedback from the speaker. Feedback in ministry may come more indirectly and with less clarity than is desirable in this exercise.

The Exercise: Set a meeting time of *at least* half an hour (an hour may be better) for *each* of you to be speaker. It is best to separate these times and not do them one after the other in a single block of time. Decide who is to be the speaker and who is to be the listener during the first time period. The reverse will be the second time—whoever was listener first will then be the speaker. *Do not meet in a public place.* Find a space where you can have some privacy, will not be interrupted by others, and where both of you feel comfortable.

During the Listening:

The speaker is the one to do *most* of the talking. As the speaker you are free to talk about anything you choose. Do not feel any pressure to talk about something you are not sure you want to share. Know that what you say is expected to be held in confidence by the listener and *not be reported in the listener's self-evaluation.* Respect the time limits upon which both of you have agreed. Notice how it feels to be heard and not heard during the exercise.

The listener should *not* feel that she or he should say *nothing*, but keep responses to efforts to let the person know you are listening, that you have heard what the speaker said. Be tuned in to how you are feeling and to what the speaker is saying. As you listen, also be assessing yourself and be aware of what distracts you or interferes with your listening in any way. Make a mental note of what distracts you, or *if the speaker has agreed*, you may make a written note. If you have the equipment, and you both agree, you may tape your conversation—audio or video. Be aware that your self-evaluation as speaker may take on many more nuances if you face yourself on tape.

Following the Listening:

Both the speaker and the listener should take a few minutes to talk about the listening (or lack thereof) that has taken place/been experienced. It is a good idea to let the listener begin with some self-assessment, and then let the speaker respond and add whatever they wish. This need not be a lengthy discussion since it is only the beginning of the evaluation process. Note that this is a reason not to do your sessions one after another in the same time period. The listener needs time to review and write down her or his self-evaluation before it gets lost in a subsequent experience.

Writing about It:

The Listener: Write approximately three pages about your experience as the listener. What interfered with your listening? What enabled your listening? How much did you talk and how did it relate to the speaker? Could you tell how the speaker felt about your listening? Include some reflections on where you need to work on your listening. When you are finished, give your paper to the speaker to read.

The Speaker: Read the listener's paper and compare the listener's self-evaluation with your experience of being heard/not heard. Write a one-page response, confirming their self-assessment, disagreeing with it, and/or adding your own reflections. Tell the listener how it felt not to be heard. Your comments need not be overly harsh (don't be mean) but should be *honestly what you experienced*. Your work here is intended to help a colleague grow in listening skills, so if you try to be nice (maybe so they will be nice to you?) you will not be helping. If the listener has done a really good job, then you have to work harder to help them grow. Give your paper to the listener and talk together about it.

If you are in a class setting, hand in both papers together for the instructor's remarks and evaluation. Be alert to what told you that the listener was not hearing you. Try to be specific and check this out with the listener. Be clear about how you felt when you felt you were not heard.

Alternative Exercise to Do by Yourself

If you are too uncomfortable to attempt the above exercise, you might want to try this one instead or as a prelude or substitute to the one above.

When you identify (or suspect) an issue that is one you clearly do not want to entertain (notice the hospitality connection), give it a little space at your table, offer it hospitality for a brief time to see if you can discern its connection to you. Its connection to you is not always immediately evident. If you are too uncomfortable with it, let it go, but promise yourself that it is something to which you will need to return for deeper understanding. It might also be possible to push yourself to do some reading in the subject area. This approach, for some, gives them enough distance to feel more comfortable with the issue. Information is a helpful tool.

Be alert to moments in your listening ministry that may bring this issue to you, and remember to keep your humility up front. There are some times to say to a speaker, "I cannot deal with this issue at this time." This is always followed with, "Here is someone who can." When we know what issues are too painful for us to help with, we must be certain to have clear and reliable referral sources right at hand. For example, child abuse and rape help resources are commonly available.

Exercise 2a: My Plan for Preparation

Think about preparing to listen to someone. Write out what you will do to prepare yourself. Develop your own ritual for getting ready to listen. Develop a prayer that you could use to be a part of your getting ready process and your ritual of preparation. If you would find it helpful, share your process and your prayer with a colleague and ask for feedback.

LISTENING FOR WHAT IS NOT BEING SAID: THOUGHTFUL AVAILABILITY IN LISTENING

Introduction

Words *do not* say it all. Beneath, beyond, between, within, and around the words that are spoken lie pools of deep meaning. These meanings are conveyed in expressions, tones, gestures, and body language. Part of the reason for these communications is that they emerge from the multiplicity of the ways in which we, as human beings, are able to communicate. Ideally, we would be able to respond to nonverbal communications openly, but that is not usually acceptable, nor are we prepared to do so. Human beings are able to communicate in many forms, but not all are acknowledged, even when they are "heard." One who truly listens must be able to tune into, to be aware of, to be willing to approach, acknowledge, and sometimes inquire about the meanings of that which is communicated but unspoken.

Listening goes beyond what the ears can receive. We constantly express ourselves in ways that words do not convey. Very subtle tones, expressions, and movements communicate to us, sometimes below the surface of our awareness. Postures and gestures carry meanings that we grasp subconsciously and instantaneously. All of these are ways of communicating that we need to be able to call into our conscious awareness

45

when we are in the listening role. Thoughtful availability enables us to tune into what is not said and recognize that unless we are willing to let ourselves "hear" and attend to these messages, we will miss a great deal in our listening role.

In chapter 1 we examined elements of hospitality as a way to get to a deeper understanding and better practice of listening. We discovered the concept of thoughtful availability as essential to the activity of hospitality. Engaging in thoughtful availability involves a watchful, attentive readiness. Thoughtful availability is a stance for both hospitality and effective listening. It makes the host accessible to the guest. The host is in a position of readiness in relation to the guest—the listener in relation to the speaker. The listener walks a path between calling out what is sensed and not spoken and intrusively violating what the speaker must, at this time, keep unspoken. Thoughtful availability enables the listener to walk that difficult way between calling out and intruding. Courage plays a role in thoughtful availability when we see and hear what we know is supposed to be ignored and choose to identify it, to call it out.

As we approach the act of listening, this stance, readiness, and attentiveness must be a part of what we provide to our guest, the speaker. Thoughtful availability makes the speaker the focus for the one who is listening. It is a particular kind of focus that includes a sense of mindfulness, which also presents the listener as accommodating. The guest/speaker and the host/listener are linked together in a "receptive alliance."[1]

The listener is in an attitude of anticipation. The listener puts aside her or his own distractions to offer the speaker thoughtful availability expressive of the servant nature of listening and hospitality. Thoughtful availability is what makes silence fruitful in the context of listening. Thoughtful availability appears to me as a gesture. The listener's hand is slightly outstretched, palm facing up, hand open. This gesture symbolizes the listener's willingness to welcome and receive whatever the speaker offers.

Pastoral care and counseling has made use of the phrase "ministry of presence" as a way of speaking about focus and attentiveness to a speaker/parishioner. For some, presence has included a sense of suffering with or alongside one who is struggling or in pain. I fear that in many cases the understanding of presence has fallen short of conveying what it intends. I think it can mean something like thoughtful availability, but it is too often heard and practiced as a matter of just being there. The value in being stands in contrast to much ministry that sees the value only in doing. Thoughtful availability can overcome a dichotomy between being and doing since it has the potential to incorporate both.

Being in thoughtful availability provides access to what needs to be done. In our welcoming offering of thoughtful availability, we are open and receptive, attentive to what may come. We hold ourselves ready for whatever may come from the speaker. We make ourselves available to hear what is not spoken in words. In hearing what is not said, we are able to lift up or call out things unspoken that may be of great value when brought to light. This calling out is an expression of *doing* in thoughtful availability.

This chapter will focus on the understanding and application of thoughtful availability in the practice of pastoral listening. Understanding thoughtful availability includes examining the role that silence plays in listening and an exploration of the importance of what is *not said* as we engage in hearing beyond the words. The image of servantship (introduced in chapter 1) is used as a way to understand thoughtful availability.

Socialization to Not Hear

We are trained, or at least we learn that we are not to pay overt attention to all that we see and hear. Civil society teaches us that it is polite sometimes to ignore what is right before our faces. As pastors, we have to begin to learn how to push aside polite and be able to hear, to have (and use) the courage to respond to what is communicated apart from words and underneath the surface of the words spoken. Being an effective listener means unlearning some of what we have been taught.

Children are sometimes taught not to stare at someone who is different, a person in a wheelchair, for example. Parents say, "Don't stare!" and turn the child away. This is a way of learning not to see. As children grow up with the experience of being told "don't look," they begin to automatically turn their heads. If we find ourselves in public in the presence of a domestic argument or a scene of a parent hitting a child, we tend to turn away. We have learned not to interfere in others' family business. We don't see what is happening right in front of us, because we have turned aside so it is no longer in front of us. Many of the things we learn not to see become linked with shame or embarrassment. We are just as likely (when we are well socialized) to turn away from too overt and too intimate expressions of affection.

You will sense the presence of polite expectations in some of the examples used to examine what is expressed beyond the words. Counseling with couples offers many opportunities for calling attention to what is being said beyond the words. In the examples that follow, the names of the speakers presented have been changed. Some of the examples are composite creations here, as well as elsewhere, in the book.

The Power of What Is Not Being Said: Martin and Grace

Years ago I was counseling a couple, Grace and Martin, when the counseling center where I was working got some new video equipment. I was excited at the opportunity to try out our new technology. I asked this couple if I could videotape our session. Midway through the session, Grace was speaking at length about their relationship. Martin was, at the same time, *whistling*.[2] I stopped the tape to rewind it and show them what had taken place. *Neither* of them had been *consciously aware* of his whistling. All of us were stunned.

Think about the message Martin was conveying to Grace while he whistled. He was not talking over her words. His communication was much more subtle. What was he saying to Grace? Take a moment out of reading this book. Put yourself in Grace's place. What message do you receive from Martin? How could his whistling communication have been related to what Grace was saying at the time? This last question cannot be answered definitively from this distance, but would be a good question to keep in mind for situations in which you see hidden communications.

This experience provided the opportunity for us to talk about communication and to deal with some deeper issues in their relationship that led to Martin's tuning out (in a very real sense) when Grace talked. I invited them to think about other times when this or something similar had happened and to be alert for other incidents that might be similar. I encouraged both of them to make use of the radar we all have, but fail to heed. I urged them to allow themselves to hear this kind of message from each other *consciously*.

I suspect that this incident in their relationship was not a one-time event, nor was it likely to have been a one-way street. Grace probably had her own ways of communicating to Martin that she was not listening. If both of them could become conscious of *all* the messages sent and received between them, their communications could vastly improve.

Tina and Carl

Tina was speaking about how Carl's family always seemed to put her down and even ignore her during events with his family. Carl shifted his position so that now he could only see Tina by looking over his shoulder. He had literally turned his back on her. He did not say a word. He did not disagree with what she was saying. He did not try to interrupt. He did not present an alternative point of view. He just simply shifted his position to turn his back toward her. This not-so-subtle move could be easily ignored by anyone listening to Carl. We have to work intentionally to "hear" this kind of communication.

Carl communicated volumes with his movement and position. If asked what it meant, he probably could have denied any awareness of his movement conveying a message. But Tina heard him loud and clear. Tina, if asked what he was saying through his new position, could tell you *what it meant to her*. The message was received. But without anyone calling attention to his movement, she probably would have left it at the subconscious level—heard and *felt*, but not named.

In every case, the pastor listening *should not presume to know what such a move means*, but leave it to Carl and Tina to define.[3] Nonverbal communications may be called to the attention of the couple by wondering about them or merely noticing. Offer responses such as, "I wonder, Tina, if you noticed Carl's movement"; or, "I see that Carl has shifted his position." These observations come out of thoughtful availability.

Sherri and Todd

Sherri and Todd offer another image. Todd is speaking about their relationship, focusing on their financial struggles—how Sherri spends money without consideration of the limits of their budget and what trouble this creates between them. Sherri is silent, but her facial expression changes the instant he mentions her spending habits. Todd does not register awareness of the change. He doesn't look directly at Sherri. Her face is clearly arranged in a scowl. A listener/observer might *assume* that she does not want him to talk about her spending habits. *Is this what she is* "saying" to Todd? We can only find out by calling her expression to the attention of both of them. It is most likely that Todd has gotten a message, whether he is conscious of it or not, whether he has looked directly at Sherri or not. With a simple act of calling his attention to what you have seen, what he "heard" subconsciously can be called to the surface for explicit expression.

Carl and Sherri might deny that there is anything to their messages. Upon your noticing, Carl will probably shift his position immediately and Sherri's scowling expression is likely to disappear. Sometimes when such communication is called to a "speaker's" attention, the response is a smile or laughter—maybe expressing relief, delight, or embarrassment at being seen and "heard." At times speakers will give clues to something important, and discovery of these clues may free the speaker to open up more of what has been hidden.

In each of these instances, the speaker may be very clear about what is being "said" by the "silent" partner. When what they *have seen*, but have not allowed themselves to register consciously, is called to their attention, often they are able to interpret accurately what they were being "told." The pastoral listener should not respond with an interpretation, but with a direction for the couple to attend to what was said. "Tina, notice how Carl is sitting. What do you understand that he is saying to you?" "Todd, Sherri is telling you something with her facial expression. What do you hear?" Or returning to an earlier situation, "Grace, what is the message you get from Martin's whistling?" Another option for questions in these instances might be addressed to the silent partner. "Sherri, how were you feeling about what Todd was saying?"

In the suggestions I have just given for response to what is seen and not expressed in words, I have offered examples of responses and sometimes following questions. My preference is to stop before asking a question— to offer an observation. "This is what I am seeing." It can be helpful to leave it there without a question, which will allow for the speaker or their partner to speak to what I describe rather than what I ask. In describing, I offer a mirror for the person or couple to look into and see their reflection. The revealing having taken place, the response does not have to be influenced by a question. As soon as a question is asked, I have begun to initiate an interpretation.

The approach of thoughtful availability allows a couple or an individual to do the work that will really help them improve the quality of their relationships. Practicing thoughtful availability, the listener is challenged to greater attentiveness that "listens" beyond the words spoken and receives messages sent, whether intentional or not, allowing for their meanings to be revealed.

Humility has been presented as an element of hospitality and listening. Here it plays an active role in the listener's awareness of not being able to *know* the meaning of the unspoken message. Whereas the unspoken message is not always clearly deciphered, the listener does know a message was sent and can participate in encouraging the "speaker" to make plain the message.

Thoughtful Availability Says, "I See You"

Many times feelings are not identified verbally. We notice a facial expression or a gesture that speaks volumes about what someone feels, but polite society tells us that we should ignore such revealing expressions. We can recognize and know a feeling (some feeling) is there but may not be able to identify it consciously.

Toby, a sixteen-year-old church member whose family was going through a lot of painful struggles, has a conversation with you. While he speaks happily about his parents you notice that he is smiling, but you also see that tears are welling up in his eyes. You have the choice of responding to his cheerful words and smiling face, or attending to the tears you see emerging. Maybe the two go together, but *you cannot guess how* if they do. Maybe you will be able to respond to both the smile and the tears.

Being polite would mean giving attention only to what Toby presents in words (maybe not his facial expressions), using his words to tell you what to give the most importance. To call attention to the tears in any way violates social rules, but offers thoughtful availability and facilitates caring. "I see your tears," may be all that needs to be said for Toby to redirect his words toward the fullness of what he is feeling. Going beyond what is normally socially acceptable makes it possible to recognize Toby at a deeper level.

However, Toby might be caught off guard by any notice to his tears and deny the tears, running away from the tears (while the tears run) and what he feels, rather than speaking it. Naming the presence of the tears is a communication of "I see you" essential to "hearing" and caring for another. This communication of seeing may be threatening for us whether we are speaker or listener when we are accustomed to traveling incognito through our lives.

To guess or imagine what is going on for Toby would be inappropriate, particularly because it is likely to be inaccurate. Let me give you some options for what could be going on that Toby expresses: Toby just got the news that his mother has cancer; his parents are getting a divorce; Toby was abused as a small child and is relieved that the family now has better times, although the hurt remains. These are widely divergent possibilities. You might immediately think of other possibilities. As you can see, it would not be possible to guess without a lot more information or Toby's own revelation about what is going on.

The Importance of "I See You"

The listener who "hears" Sherri and Carl and responds to what was not spoken is saying, "I see you" to them. The message "I see you" is extremely powerful. I suspect part of this power lies in our not feeling *seen* very often, even by those who know us well. When someone says, "I see you," I feel more like I matter.

The power of "I see you" enters our lives when we are infants. Adults mirror the sounds and expressions babies make. We do this anticipating a mirroring back by the baby. We speak to babies in their "native tongue" as we mirror or reflect back to them their baby sounds. We also witness the power of the game of peek-a-boo. Babies learn to hide using their blankets, by ducking behind a parent's head, or by putting their hands over their eyes in order to experience the delight of being "discovered" again by the adult who has joined them in the game. This is a game of "I see you," learned from our earliest days of life. The delight of this discovery lasts long into childhood. Maybe it has never gone away.

It is easy, in the lives of many people, to feel insignificant and even invisible. Our invisibility or insignificance is reinforced by the many times when "listeners" do not hear us. We long to be seen and heard.[4] The story of Zacchaeus illustrates the insignificance that many people experience: Even though Zacchaeus was a tax collector with some power and wealth, he experienced little esteem from the people of Jericho. He wanted to see who Jesus was and, being a short man, climbed a tree so he could see past the crowd.

When Jesus came to the place, he looked up and said to him, "Zacchaeus, hurry and come down; for I must stay at your house today." So he hurried down and was happy to welcome him. All who saw it began to grumble and said, "He has gone to be the guest of one who is a sinner." Zacchaeus stood there and said to the Lord, "Look, half of my possessions, Lord, I will give to the poor; and if I have defrauded anyone of anything, I will pay back four times as much." Then Jesus said to him, "Today salvation has come to this house, because he too is a son of Abraham. For the Son of Man came to seek out and to save the lost." (Luke 19:5-10)

The power of communicating "I see you" transformed Zacchaeus's life. By *seeing* him, Jesus held up a mirror and Zacchaeus saw himself. Zacchaeus was able to become who he truly was, a son of Abraham.

"I see you" still has this power today. When we *see* someone and allow what we presume to be polite or correct to keep us from acknowledging who we see, the person remains unseen and unheard. We realize the response that we make to the spoken words may not convey that we have truly seen or heard, especially when we ignore the *unspoken* messages.

It is both frightening and a relief to be seen and heard. A person acting as a speaker may leap to deny what a listener hears that the speaker feels is socially unacceptable. Toby may be ashamed, as a teenaged male, to admit he is crying; or he might be ashamed of the story the tears are exposing. At the same time he may be deeply relieved to have someone willing to walk into the room with him where he has left the door only ajar.

In "hearing" and noticing what is unspoken, when we risk saying "I see you," we need to be willing to allow the avoidance of the speaker when it seems necessary for that person, at that time. To insist that I "heard" something when the speaker denies that there is any unspoken message can be intrusive and become a violation rather than true listening. We can remind ourselves that this is one time on the journey with the person and there can be other times in the future. If I remain thoughtfully available in my relationship with this person, the message may be made clear another time. My listening will have paid off in the healing it can offer for pain that is right now too sore to touch or too ugly to expose.

Jesus, lying at the table at Simon's house, asked Simon, "Do you see this woman?" (Luke 7:44). Of course Simon saw the woman. She was the source of Simon's muttering against Jesus, which Jesus began to address as he posed an earlier question to Simon about which debtor would love the forgiving creditor more (v. 42). The question, "Do you see this woman?" called everyone's attention to the woman who was behind Jesus washing his feet. She was offering to Jesus hospitality neglected by Simon, the host.

When Jesus asked this question, the roles of host and guest shifted. Jesus became the host to the woman who was offering him hospitality. He demonstrated thoughtful availability toward her at this point. Asking the question "Do you see this woman?" made it clear that Jesus *did* "see" the woman, even though her position was behind him. In this position, she would have been much more visible to Simon. Yet, Jesus asked Simon, "Do you see this woman?" underscoring that Simon did not really see her, but rather only who or what he thought or *presumed* her to be, unclean and a sinner. Once again Simon failed in his role as host when he neglected to see the woman for who she was.

Thoughtful availability leads the host to affirm the presence of the guest, to be aware of the guest. Jesus did not hesitate to call everyone's attention to the woman. She had provided thoughtful availability to Jesus and he responded in kind. Jesus clearly saw her, and in his speech to Simon he was clear that he saw what she did, the meaning of which Simon had entirely missed.

Thoughtful Availability in Process as Well as Content

In listening with thoughtful availability we not only experience *what* is said, but also *how* it is said. We listen to content and process. We have explored nonverbal communications and here we find another dimension. The way in which something is said, even aside from tone and expression, opens up what we might hear beyond the words spoken. The spoken message apart from the process does not give us the entire message.

Myron Chartier described a family incident that is extremely revealing regarding communication of unintentional messages:

> A few years ago my daughter was watching a preacher on television. Suddenly she asked, "Dad, what's he mad about?" Since I was reading the paper, I didn't really know, but after observing for a while, I said, "Melody, I don't know why he's angry or with whom he is angry. He's

preaching about love!" The intended message was love, but the unintended nonverbal message was anger.[5]

The sermon was about love, but the way the message was being communicated was saying anger. Apparently Chartier's daughter heard the unintended message much more clearly than the intended message. The process spoke louder than the words.

Mack has been talking to his pastor for a while. Nothing remarkable has come up in the conversation, even though Mack had made an appointment to have the conversation. Mack is on the way out the door and pauses for a moment, saying, "By the way . . ." The "by the way" as he is almost out the door alerts the pastor that what is to follow deserves attention. "By the way" delivered in this manner is an expression of ambivalence about what the speaker wants (and doesn't want) to say. By placing the content in the position of being an afterthought, Mack expresses hesitancy at bringing it up at all. Underlying his hesitation are likely to be feelings of vulnerability related to whatever follows "by the way." The pastor sees that this is what Mack really came to talk about and is ready to give it the focus Mack has tried to avoid (even though Mack made the appointment).

Thoughtful availability enables the pastor to refocus on this new topic or information that Mack now brings, with awareness of Mack's need for some distance or safety regarding the topic. Thoughtful availability enables the pastor to recognize there is something of importance here. The pastor is able to encourage Mack to sit down again and go further into what he has mentioned. If the pastor's time is too limited at this point (a subconscious goal Mack held), it is possible to immediately schedule another time to meet and explicitly identify Mack's new issue as the focus for the conversation.

In thoughtful availability, the pastor joins with the speaker's impulse toward resolution and healing, which is expressed at times in process rather than in the words spoken. Our first inclination might be to enable Mack to avoid what he has successfully avoided during the whole conversation, but this is not where thoughtful availability takes us. We choose the side of his ambivalence that seeks healing.

Attending to process is another piece of thoughtful availability. What comes to us in words has to be understood in its context of body language, gesture, expression, tone, and process. We do not get the full meaning without these revealing communications.

Thoughtful Availability as Servantship

When we accept the traditional foundation for ministry as leadership, we will find ourselves in a position of listening that differs from one of thoughtful availability. When I see myself as leader, I may be more inclined to want to fix a situation or give an answer for a struggle a parishioner faces. Servantship provides a contrasting image that allows for thoughtful availability, a readiness to receive and respond rather than direct and lead. Today's predominant society does not tend to value service as much as it does leadership. Leadership means power and control, and this image has entered the church as an important model for ministry.

Servantship gets some powerful support from Jesus. In a story with which we may not be comfortable, Jesus unmistakably places himself in a servant—even subservient—position by washing the feet of his disciples. Some churches reenact the practice of foot washing that Jesus practiced with his disciples. Many other churches ignore the practice.

> Jesus, knowing that the Father had given all things into his hands, and that he had come from God and was going to God, got up from the table, took off his outer robe, and tied a towel around himself. Then he poured water into a basin and began to wash the disciples' feet and to wipe them with the towel that was tied around him. He came to Simon Peter, who said to him, "Lord, are you going to wash my feet?" Jesus answered, "You do not know now what I am doing, but later you will understand." Peter said to him, "You will never wash my feet.". . . After he had washed their feet, had put on his robe, and had returned to the table, he said to them, "Do you know what I have done to you? You call me Teacher and Lord—and you are right, for that is what I am. So if I, your Lord and Teacher, have washed your feet, you also ought to wash one another's feet. For I have set you an example, that you also should do as I have done to you." (John 13:3-7, 12-15)

Jesus not only presents to the disciples the image of being a servant to them, but he also makes it perfectly clear that they are to follow his example with one another. Obviously, as their Lord and Teacher, Jesus did not see it as beneath himself to act as a servant to his disciples. Apart from the act of foot washing being an act of hospitality, here it becomes a visual and tactile lesson for the disciples. Being servants to one another is elevated to an honorable practice and expectation.

Jesus comes to this act out of a perspective on himself that we might note. Jesus got up from the table with the clear intention to wash the disciples' feet *knowing* that God had given "all things into his hands, and that he had come from God and was going to God" (v. 3). When Jesus came to Peter, Peter did not want his Lord to wash his feet. It seems that Peter wanted Jesus to stay in his role as the leader and not act as servant to him. Jesus came to this role out of a clear sense of who he was, where he was from, and where he was going. Jesus was able to incorporate a role that meant humility without losing his identity as Lord and Teacher.

We receive from Jesus the clear affirmation of an ability to step into the role of service to others maintaining the clarity he had on who he was and where he was going. The servantship quality of thoughtful availability has a place in our listening service to others.

Beyond the Nonverbal as We Know It

We tend to think of nonverbal communication in terms of body language like in the situations that have been presented above. The nonverbal takes other forms in situations in which there is a message to be heard, but it appears not in words or in actions.

A young woman, a member of the church where she was married only two years earlier, seeks a conversation with the pastor. Immediately when she enters the pastor's study, he sees she has a serious black eye. They begin to talk and after a while the conversation turns to Judy's feelings about how jealous her husband has been. Pastor Mark assures Judy that he can understand how her husband could be jealous of "such a pretty young wife." The conversation continues until finally, well into the conversation, Judy finally says, "My husband did this to me," indicating her black eye.

Without going further in their conversation I want to point out how Pastor Mark did not listen to Judy. Her bruised face was screaming out a message. However, the pastor would have been unjustified to jump in with, "Did your husband hit you?" when he first saw the bruise. Instead, he could have said to Judy, in any number of ways, "I see you," without interpreting what he saw. Merely saying, as soon as he noticed it, "I see you have a black eye" would have allowed for Judy to feel immediately that she could talk about what had happened. By ignoring the black eye, Pastor Mark communicated some reluctance to talk about whatever it was (or whatever he suspected) that had caused the damage.

Another possibility might have been that Pastor Mark, upon seeing the black eye, would have exclaimed, "What happened to you?" This response does say "I see you," but it also bends the conversation toward judgment. Pastor Mark can say to Judy that he sees her without asking a question that leaves it to Judy to tell him what happened or not. The question demands a particular answer, an explanation. An observation that he sees the black eye is all that is necessary to let Judy know that he would be willing to talk about it. Pastor Mark is not there to do an investigation. He is there to receive Judy and offer her caring as her pastor.

In a conversation report about this incident, Pastor Mark explained that he waited to see if Judy would mention the black eye. I suspect he didn't want to get into it. He had performed her wedding. Judy's mother was a core church member. He didn't want Judy to tell him what her face was saying to him. In polite society we avoid calling attention to something like this obvious bruise. The pastor might have suspected spousal abuse, and could not imagine dealing with that, particularly since he had participated in joining Judy and her husband together, possibly with some sense of misgiving.

What we are willing to listen to that does not come in words or in actions or expressions may be determined in part by what we have been prepared to face by our training or by our personal experience. Personal experience can be a mixed bag in dealing with painful issues like violence. If we carry wounds from our lives that have not been adequately healed, we may not be able to reach out to allow a speaker to identify their pain.

However, when we have painful experiences that have been adequately healed, these past experiences can become an asset in our listening. The successful listening encouraged in Twelve-Step programs such as Alcoholics Anonymous and Al Anon demonstrates the value past experiences can bring to enable healing in others when the one helping has been adequately healed. Self-awareness is essential for the thoughtful availability of naming what we *see* in our practice of listening. The courage necessary in practicing thoughtful availability that notices and names is essential in the practice of ministry.

Subtexts

We have seen that running underneath the spoken words of conversations are what might be called subtexts. They are consistently important messages, but messages that are not given words. Self-awareness of the listener allows more room for hearing these messages. Self-awareness of the speaker may not be sufficient for the speaker to have full knowledge of his or her own subtexts or even a clue that these subtexts are running underneath what the person is saying.

Thoughtful availability enables us to give the subtexts some attention and presents an opportunity for the speaker to see a subtext he or she may not have recognized. In all of the examples given throughout this chapter we have discovered the existence of subtexts, but we have not always been able to tell just what their messages were. Awareness of their existence and recognition that their contents may prove valuable for the speaker, when they are raised to the surface, is a part of the role of the effective listener.

Silence in Thoughtful Availability

We tend to make use of silence to do our own work—to think of what we will say next, or how we can solve the problem presented or search for what answer would be appropriate to give the speaker. We see silence as a space to be filled and, at our worst, an opportunity to gain control. We use silence to interject our own stories. Silence is much more valuable when it is used for other purposes. Silence provides space for the speaker to do nonverbal work. It allows for attending to the voice of God as well as to internal voices that may have something to add to what has been said. It is space for reflection on what has taken place, for reception of new insights, and assimilation of what has been revealed. Silence is not empty, not an absence, but an activity. Silence is not nothing happening, nor is it time wasted. Silence is more like a fertile field ready for something to sprout.

The listener uses silence well by actively remaining focused on the speaker, being open and thoughtfully available and attentive. Expectation and anticipation keep the listener available for the next words that may come. The listener is not detached, not closed, not turned inward and self-preoccupied. In silence the level of the listener's comfort is most important. The listener is in the mode of receiving in allowing silence to exist. Silence is an ongoing welcome, an offer of hospitality when it is used in these ways. The mental gesture remains as an open hand, palm facing up, slightly extended toward the silent speaker—not in a demanding way, but in a receiving gesture.

Listeners struggle with silence when we feel it means a loss of control or a failure of ability as a listener. The listener suspects that the speaker feels that the listener may be inept, simply because there is silence. We have strong tendencies to break silence with questions—our efforts to get the speaker to talk. Most of the time only a few seconds pass before a listener jumps in to speak.[6] This uneasiness with silence can demonstrate a lack of faith in the speaker and in the listening process. We feel the need to provide an answer because we do not recognize the work that is being done during the silence. We do not recognize that the silent "speaker" is often doing his or her own work in our presence during the silence. Silence allows for the deepest parts of ourselves to bubble up, which can happen for the listener as well as the speaker. Some fear of what might come up causes us to terminate silence prematurely. We demonstrate a lack of faith in our failure to expect that the Holy Spirit may well be at work in the silence. The Holy Spirit does indeed work without our words. In silence anything can happen.

Groh's image of receptive alliance between speaker and listener leads me to the image of our being joined in receptivity toward God. Our alliance has a focus beyond both of us. We are together in thoughtful availability in the presence of God with silence providing it a context.

Courage in Thoughtful Availability

On the surface thoughtful availability does not seem to be a function that requires courage. This impression is mistaken and misleading. We have seen that it takes courage to violate the commonly held social agreements not to notice and not to name what people avoid speaking directly.

We speak about calling out messages that have come disguised in an action, expression, tone, or condition. It takes courage to call out those feelings that are left unnamed. It takes courage to hear painful feelings—to listen to horrible life experiences, to face the depths of fear, grief, and anger of the speaker when we have provided the space for them to speak by providing thoughtful availability. It takes courage to stay focused on a person whose feelings are scary as we sit together in silence.

For Pastor Mark to recognize that Judy came to his office with a black eye—for him to speak this—is an act of courage. Everything about her having a black eye was something he would have chosen to avoid. It was threatening to him, for the church, to acknowledge to Judy that he saw the black eye. To deeply explore the issues around her being hit by her husband posed even more threat to his feelings—about relationships between women and men, about divorce, about the community finding out and his ministry being judged. To notice (to see) takes courage.

When we choose to ignore or avoid nonverbal communications or conditions presented to us in the person who comes as the speaker, we must give our focus to the question of whose needs are being met in the avoidance. When we see the threats for Pastor Mark, and we notice that he does not name her black eye, it seems like his own needs have taken priority over Judy's needs. This is a major issue in listening. Defending ourselves makes thoughtful availability impossible. Our attentiveness to the speaker is severely limited when our concern takes a shift in focus toward ourselves as the listeners.

Feeling some threat to ourselves does not have to lead to an entire failure of courage, but can call our attention, briefly, to what is presenting a threat to us and what it is threatening. Once we can identify what the threat is, we are better able to put it aside and return our availability to the speaker.

Thoughtful Availability in the Midst of Clouded Waters

Thoughtful availability may be our tool of access to those moments in listening when the speaker floods us with words and we find ourselves in danger of drowning in too many words with too little focus. What is the message in the midst of all of these words? I know there is something important there, but the speaker's words have thrashed about in the waters so much that nothing is clear. The water has been clouded with so much action of so many words. We are left sorting through what appear to be meaningless piles of words. The speaker seemed to start out on one direction and then shifted from that to another and then another. We got lost. We began to suffer from a need for silence.

Thoughtful availability allows us to wait and receive. In receiving we may be able to enable the speaker to find a focus. Invite the speaker to pause: "Let's slow down for a moment. I need some help with a focus here." At such a moment touch might be helpful. Placing a hand on the forearm of the speaker may contribute to slowing things down, getting the speaker's attention, and finding a break in the stream. The listener could add, "These are some of the things I have heard you saying (rewording what has been heard as central in all that has been said), but I am still not clear on where you are heading."

Hearing It Again: A Painful Moment in Ministry[7]

As the pastor of a local congregation, you are making a visit to the nearby nursing home where some of your church members are residents. The woman you are visiting has begun to tell you the same long story she has repeated almost every time you have visited, even before she came to the nursing home. To listen to it again is downright painful. You realize how much is waiting for your attention—holidays approaching, a sermon to write, phone calls to return—the list is endless. This list is the reason behind why today is your first visit here in three months. After a while you try to offer a shortcut to the story being told by jumping ahead to mention a point you know will be coming up. It doesn't work. You plan an outline for the agenda of the board meeting scheduled tonight. You've heard the story word for word. You don't have to listen again, you convince yourself.

Allow me to interrupt: I want to suggest something. There may be a gift in there—in all that you have heard again and again. There may be a gift for you or one for the speaker, or even gifts for both of you. Take the challenge to try to find it. That means listening more closely than before, listening intently for places where there may be gaps in the story or where the transition is not clear or doesn't make sense. It means asking for the speaker to focus more closely on those points and tell you more.

Suddenly you see something new. There is a surprise for you in what you are hearing, an insight for the person who has spoken this story so many times trying to find what she has now discovered. "So that is why I had to keep telling that story! There was something there I needed to find, to recognize. I was that close so many times, I feel certain, but I needed you to hear me so I could find it."

You, as listener, have become party to the new birth that this found connection delivers. This could be the story of countless people. Their stories need thoughtful availability and not just the endurance to get through it again, which can be a listener's reaction.

The kind of expectation that says "something can be found here" doesn't happen when we are afraid or feel insecure in our listening. When we approach listening with fears, we expect a threatening experience. What if this person experiencing pain, life tragedy, or struggle brings something that may challenge what I believe? I find ways to keep that from happening when I think of ways to preempt their searching and give them a "correct theological approach" to their situation. Or perhaps, I offer them, "Let's pray about that" before they have even finished telling the whole story.

Coming to the act of listening with a clear attitude of expectation, what might we discover in this experience? What will God bring? This kind of expectation, rooted in thoughtful availability, enables us to be open, eager searchers who are ready to receive something unexpected, and to become listeners who have the faith to trust that the grace of God is available to play a role in the discovery.

Conclusion

Effective listening requires the thoughtful availability and attentiveness that makes it possible for us to see and "hear" what is not said. As much as people want to be seen, we also struggle with tension between revealing and hiding what we feel and being exposed by what we show. The listener is challenged to be alert and available in order to catch the clues given that will enable both the listener and the speaker to discover deeper levels of "speaking" and revealing. It is much easier to ignore the unspoken than to bring it forward and follow where it leads us with the speaker. The journey may be difficult for both the speaker and the listener.

The next chapter will focus on the struggle for the listener as well as the speaker to move forward into areas of vulnerability that come with the territory of speaking and listening. We are aware that feeling vulnerable is a threat for listeners and speakers alike. Our level of comfort in our listening role may contribute to the speaker feeling less vulnerable, along with ourselves.

Focus Questions/Actions

Think of ways in which you can communicate "I see you" to someone who is speaking. Notice times when you have "seen" some message that you have not "called out" for the attention of the speaker. How might you do that on another occasion? Be prepared by making some choices before you need them. Practicing a "listening prayer" may be a way to prepare oneself to be silent and available. Be in an attitude of thoughtful availability and focus on God for a time of prayer. Be clear that you are ready to receive what God has for you. When there is silence in a conversation, pay attention to how it feels to you. Can you feel comfortable? Be aware of what is going on for you, what you are doing during the silence. Do you feel any anxiety? Are you planning ahead for your next response?

Exercise 3: Silence in Listening

Introduction: One of the greatest difficulties in listening is being able to tolerate silence. The listener who sees him or herself in the role of the caregiver takes on responsibility for the conversation. What this responsibility means to us is that we carry the burden for keeping the person talking—keeping the conversation going. When there is silence we may experience a fear of failure, anxiety about not "doing our job" well or not being helpful. We recognize that silence leaves the door open for almost anything to happen. We feel increasing need to fill the void and encourage the speaker to *say something*.

So much in our everyday lives defies the existence of silence—background noise, music, cell phone use, the sound of traffic, airplanes, machinery. Many people leave radios and televisions on even when they are not listening or watching. Perhaps it is getting more difficult for us to live with silence.

Exercise Part A

Schedule time and an appropriate place (where you will not be distracted). Half an hour is a minimum amount of time. Arrange for a conversation with a partner. You will be the listener (who also responds). Focus on what your partner says and also on your own comfort with silence. Be aware of moments of discomfort during silence and pay attention to what you do at those times. Neither of you should try to fill all of the space with words. Allow for periods of silence, and monitor how you feel in these moments. Be alert during times of silence keeping your focus on the speaker. Expectant waiting could be something you practice during silence. Remember the intent of thoughtful availability.

Exercise Part B

Select another setting. When you feel you *must say something*, pause, reflect. It is usually only a matter of a few seconds before participants make a response to what has been said or asked. Allow silence to have some space. Within a group try to sense what happens in the space the silence provides. You might notice that there are particular people who speak out whenever there is a noticeable period of silence.

Use a journal format or write a paper responding with focus on your feelings and reactions to silence. What do you think about? What do you feel? How do you do with silence in your conversations with God or in prayers? We often give God no opportunity to respond. Are you able to be silent in the presence of God? Silence is not a matter of just not talking, but also of thoughtful availability.

Exercise 3a: Not Asking Questions

Introduction: One of the common ways we deal with discomfort with silence is to ask questions. This is an exercise to increase your awareness of asking questions. The object is to not ask *any* questions, and to think of another way to encourage the speaker to go on. Questions are also asked a great deal just because the listener feels the need for additional information, or perhaps wants to seem to be doing something while the other is speaking. Prepare ahead of time by thinking of phrases or approaches you can use to encourage the speaker to continue. Sometimes we do not even wait for there to be silence and we are ready to encourage the speaker to continue, so also prepare to allow for some silence.

The Exercise: This exercise could be done with a partner from class or on your own, if you have a ministry setting in which you would have the opportunity to listen to someone. If you do it with someone in the class you will have the opportunity for guided feedback. If you do it on your own, you will have the opportunity to deal with a real situation. Either one would be useful.

During a set period of time (no less than thirty minutes and no more than an hour) listen to your speaker with awareness of your urge to ask questions. Be consistent in stopping yourself from asking questions, no matter how curious you are or how important the information you seek seems to be. Put all questions aside in your mind and keep your focus on what the speaker is saying.

Written Assignment: Briefly evaluate your ability to avoid asking questions. It is likely that you did not succeed 100 percent, but do not give excuses for the questions you asked. Think about what you asked and what the question was in relation to the whole of what the speaker had to say to you. Where you did succeed and overcome an urge to ask questions? Reflect on the questions you really wanted to ask in light of the entire conversation. What did you learn about where your questions were coming from?

If you did this exercise with a classmate, following the allotted time of speaking and listening, ask for their feedback about the questions you asked and mention to them the questions you avoided, asking also for their feedback. You may incorporate insights from this conversation in your written assignment.

Bonus Exercise: Trying to Avoid Asking Questions

Introduction: One very difficult thing many people in ministry experience is the urge to keep someone talking. The ordinary way this urge is dealt with is to ask question after question. We even succeed in training folk to wait for the questions before they go on speaking. It is as though we communicate that if we get enough answers to questions we will have an answer to solve the problem or heal the struggle. This exercise encourages you to function as a listener *without asking questions*. True, some questions may be very helpful, but we do too much question asking and need to practice ways to respond that are not in the form of questions.

Getting Ready: Prepare by having a partner and setting up appropriate space and times for each of you to have the opportunity to be the speaker and each to be the listener. Your responsibility in the role of the listener will be *not to ask any questions*. Your speaker partner can help by not talking on and on, but rather allowing times for you to respond. Your objective as the listener is to enable the speaker to continue talking and be able to tell you more about the issues the speaker has chosen to discuss.

The Exercise: Listener, be alert to avoid asking questions. When you want to respond find another way to respond. For example, practice repeating *in your own words* an important point that the speaker has made (not just any words spoken, but something that seems to be at the heart of the matter). What you are trying to do is to let the speaker know you heard, and encourage the speaker to continue. Other suggestions might be: "That really hurt"; or "Say more"; or "Go on." All of these responses avoid questions and encourage the speaker to continue. Don't forget the option to put what has been said in your own words. Doing this may encourage the speaker to continue.

The speaker is asked *not to answer* any questions that you might accidentally ask. The speaker is also helpful when she or he allows some silence before continuing to another point. Give your listener some time to be able to respond.

Reverse roles and repeat the exercise. Be sure to take some time to give each other feedback on your experience of the exercise. How painful was it to have to avoid asking questions? This is another good opportunity to write reflections in your listening journal.

CHAPTER FOUR

LISTENER BEWARE: VULNERABILITY IN LISTENING

Introduction

We have seen that it is not easy to do effective listening. At the heart of the difficulties of listening lies what is perhaps the most powerful impediment to really hearing another—vulnerability. We saw in chapter 1 how offering hospitality makes the host vulnerable. We also know that the guest who enters the scene as the one who stands in need of hospitality is already vulnerable. In addition, we noted that guests unexpectedly change the lives of their hosts. Vulnerability in listening offers the same possibilities as it does in hospitality.

We have trouble with vulnerability because it feels like weakness, like being exposed and unprotected. These possibilities are unwelcome. We are reluctant to open ourselves to feeling weak or exposed, even when we recognize that vulnerability is the only route to intimacy, effective listening, and personal growth. The odd thing about vulnerability causing us to feel weak is that no one can be vulnerable without being strong.

In acts of listening, as in acts of hospitality, host and guest, listener and speaker must be open to each other for hospitality or listening to occur. A potential host unwilling to be vulnerable will not be able to offer hospitality. In fearing vulnerability, a potential guest will be reluctant to *receive* hospitality. Likewise, welcoming and receiving another person by listening to them requires the listener to be open. When I truly listen to another with openness, I become *vulnerable*. I become vulnerable because authentic hearing brings me into intimacy with the speaker. What I hear is received into my self and is likely to affect me and probably change me. Being vulnerable to change is not always easy to entertain.

If I want to remain unchanged in contact with others, it behooves me *to avoid really hearing* what others have to say, especially when issues of great concern are spoken. The deeper the issue's importance or the more conflicted the issue, the scarier the intimacy and stronger the feelings of vulnerability involved in listening become. When we are in touch with the full reality of our vulnerability in listening, we tend to resist openly listening to another who shares deeply.

When we become vulnerable in truly listening to the other, we let go of the reins of control. We cannot be completely in charge, because listening takes us where the other person goes and not where we would want them to go, where we imagine they will go, or where we think they should go. In listening we necessarily follow where the speaker takes us. How am I going to know whether I want to go there? Will the speaker touch a place of anger, pain, fear, regret, grief, or threat felt by the listener? What might I have to face in myself as I listen to the other's pains and struggles? Will something come as a challenge to my faith? Am I prepared for what will come my way?

Listeners need to recognize that the speaker who shares openly also becomes vulnerable. The speaker, as guest, places her or himself in the care of the listener/host, relying on that being a place that will be safe. The listener, in turn, accepts responsibility for the safety of the speaker, and for what is spoken, to protect it and hold it with respect.

This chapter explores the many ways in which the pastor who listens effectively will experience or discover vulnerability. We return to recall the vulnerability Abraham, Sarah, Lot, and the gracious woman at Simon's house experienced in offering hospitality. We will see how listening involves similar vulnerability when we are open to others. There are dangers in listening of which we need to be aware in order to be able to function as effective listeners. We need to be conscious of dangers when we function as listeners. The awareness of our vulnerability may lead us to put extra effort into maintaining control of the conversation, offering premature reassurance, or giving answers. We may be comfortable with some degree of vulnerability, but when we feel like it is too much we tend to rush to protect ourselves at the same time that we think we are caring for the one who is the speaker.

Vulnerability of the Listener

In chapter 1 we became familiar with the biblical accounts of the strangers whom Lot welcomed into his home and the woman who offered Jesus the hospitality that was omitted by the host, Simon the Pharisee. In these stories we could see that Lot and the woman became vulnerable by providing hospitality to those in need—the strangers and Jesus, respectively.

The vulnerability Lot's family experienced was particularly threatening. By providing hospitality to the strangers, Lot and his family were placed in danger by the citizens of Sodom who wanted Lot to hand over the strangers for them to do with as they wished. Obeying the rules of hospitality, Lot refused to send his guests out to the mob. The guests, in return, were able to rescue Lot from the people when the mob tried to drag him off. They ultimately saved Lot from the destruction of Sodom.

The woman at Simon's house had the audacity to "play the host" to Jesus when Simon had neglected showing the basics of hospitality to Jesus as his invited guest. Her audacity included washing Jesus' feet with her tears, anointing his feet with ointment, and letting her hair down and using it to dry his feet. Her behavior was incomprehensible. She, in a sense, shamed Simon for not fulfilling the necessities of hospitality. Her life was not put in danger, but she endured the disdain of the Pharisees attending the event. The religious leaders shamed her for her thoughtful behavior.

Listening has its way of placing the host/listener in a vulnerable position. Like hospitality, listening involves being open and welcoming to the guest who is the speaker. This same openness that made the host vulnerable also makes the listener vulnerable, as we will see throughout this chapter. The listener's role also places him or her in the position of protecting the speaker, in ways that we will explore. Effective listening exposes the listener to vulnerable feelings and dangerous issues. I argue that listening is still worth the risk. The benefits to the speaker and the blessings for the listener truly make the vulnerability and risk worthwhile. At all times in listening, the safety of the speaker is the primary concern.

The thoughts and feelings placed in trust at the moment in which they are spoken are received and treated with respect. The pastoral listener is careful to not use what is heard for any purpose that could be hurtful to the speaker or to others who are related to the speaker. Nor can the listener, so entrusted, use what the speaker has spoken in any way to enhance himself or herself. What is entrusted at one time is left with the listener for a longer period of trust. The listener must keep in confidence what has been said (in most cases).

In all three of the stories of offering hospitality to strangers, besides the dangers of offering hospitality, we discovered the vulnerability of hosts to change brought about by their guests. The lives of each of the prominent characters in our stories changed dramatically because of the hospitality they provided. Offering the hospitality of listening causes one to become vulnerable to change in one's self or one's life. When we are open to what the speaker/guest brings to us, we are vulnerable to change in our lives. If we want to avoid any change, we do not want to listen deeply to another, for change will come with the listening.

Dennis Groh offers us a blatant reminder of the inevitability of vulnerability in hospitality, which we will also see in listening:

> An unexpected visitor brings the possibility of sudden and, perhaps, dramatic change to a settled household. It presents to people whose agendas are mostly known and anticipated a moment of potential change, and that almost always means of potential danger. Are the stranger's intentions friendly or ominous? Will the visitor be a friend with a delightful surprise or a menacing presence bearing an unknown hostility?[1]

There is no way to know what a speaker brings to the moment of listening.

The concern of the listener for the safety of the speaker is not held as the sole concern. The loss of the listener's safety will be costly to the listening process and, therefore, to the speaker.

Vulnerability in Responding in Listening

Responding to someone to whom I am listening is a risk. Have I heard correctly? Am I listening well? Did I hear what was important? Will my response be clearly understandable? When I give a response, I become vulnerable because I reveal myself. My response may be far from what was said. It may have *more of myself* in it than the speaker. Asking a question poses no such vulnerability. I am able to maintain a safe distance and remain relatively risk free.

As we respond we want to assure the listener that we are listening and have gotten the heart of what they have said. In our eagerness to reassure the speaker of our listening, we may make use of connections to our lives in what the speaker said. "That is just like my experience." Use caution, because our care in listening is not reflected in the number of connections we are able to make with what the speaker says. When we use connections in this way, we are avoiding feeling the vulnerability of being unsure about our listening. Our attentiveness is not appropriately fixed on the speaker when we are busy seeking out connections in our lives that we can share.

Responding by using the same words the speaker has used may not assure the speaker or confirm for the listener that the speaker has been heard rightly. One exercise I have used in class includes an exchange between a woman and her pastor in which she tells the pastor that she is "involved" with another man. To respond, "So you're involved with someone else," and get her affirmation tells you nothing about whether you have heard what she *meant* by "involved." Or you might assume that what she means is sexual involvement, although that is not what she said and may not be what she means.

When you have put what she said in your own words, you can find out whether you are with her in the conversation. In this case, responding might invite her to say more about what "involved" means to her, to help you get on the same page with her. Although some people who do counseling like to use the phrase, "Do I hear you saying. . . ?" I find this phrase to be very outdated and wonder how people hear it from a listener. I recommend not using it.

How Much Can I Bear?

When pastors listen effectively to the struggles and pain of many people, they can get to the point of feeling overburdened. Pastors who reliably keep the confidences with which they have been entrusted end up knowing a great deal about those who have spoken to them. They have heard the pains, struggles, burdens, griefs, and secrets of speakers. Usually, they know a great deal as well about others who are connected with those to whom they have listened. Carrying what we have heard is a way of bearing one another's burdens. What do listening pastors do with all that they have heard and all that they carry in confidence? How does the listening pastor manage to hold all the pain that he or she has received?

Carrying others' burdens has the effect of creating feelings of vulnerability. Our feelings are touched and disturbed, and our concern for the speaker is deep. These are dimensions of our being vulnerable. Through our listening, we are aware of the accumulation of burdens carried by many others.

On occasions when pastors recognize that the burdens they are carrying from listening are too great, this is the time to seek out or pay a visit to a professional consultant or supervisor who can offer the support the pastor needs, perhaps for a short period of time. Pastors who carry heavy burdens of many individuals within the congregation find support from God through prayer to be an essential resource. Prayers for individuals and families in need support the pastor's listening and caring ministry. It is also appropriate to bring issues you hold in confidence to professionals who are experienced in the supervision and care of pastors. A small group of ministers may decide to form a group to receive ongoing support and supervision under the guidance of a professional pastoral counselor or supervisor. Local hospitals and counseling centers may have such professionals on staff.

It is best to have some kind of support in place before it is needed in a moment of burnout or a state of being overstressed. Under the stress of the burdens one is bearing that have become excessive, one does not need added stress of trying to locate or identify a trusted listener.

Hospice programs set a good example in providing time for workers to talk together about each loss as it occurs. Being able to talk about one's burdens doesn't merely spread them around, but has the effect of easing the burdens. When they can be shared (professionally) the level of stress does not accumulate as much.

There can be too much stress from carrying the many confidences of the congregation. When pastors have strong and reliable support systems they may not feel the stress as being as debilitating as it can be when there is insufficient support. The amount we can carry is not always consistent. At some times we are able to bear much more than we can at other times. It is not realistic to expect ourselves to always function at the same capacity.

Pastors have an additional resource available that can be cultivated and become effective. That resource is the community of the congregation. The burdened pastoral listener has the possibility of working with the people, by example and through education, to help them develop their skills in listening. Parishioners who have been prepared to be effective listeners can be valued visitors to the sick and shut-in members of the congregation.

I doubt if there is anything that prompts persons to efforts of careful listening more quickly than having been listened to effectively. The congregation as a whole can come to value the gift of listening and provide for one another good resources of listening. When the community as a whole practices good listening, the need for the pastor to hear everything is diminished dramatically. The people of the congregation do not take on pastoral roles, but every Christian can become a healing listener.

Limits to Listening

We have just looked at issues of becoming overly stressed with carrying burdens of much listening to heavy issues and concerns. It is obvious that listening pastors cannot do an indefinite amount of listening. It may be important to examine a few issues related to limiting listening.

In any one situation we are only able to listen for a certain length of time. This time may vary according to the situation, but eventually, in any situation, our listening abilities will begin to dim. We begin to "check out" because the listening we have been doing is the hard work we know it to be and we have been doing our listening intently for, perhaps, an hour. We need a break. Deep and intense listening focus can only be sustained over a limited time period. To identify an hour as a time limit for listening is quite arbitrary, but it could be useful to have some sense of where our limits may fall. Placing a limit on the length of time we will listen may have the benefit of communicating to the speaker that their issue is manageable—it can be contained and dealt with. The length of time we are able to do intense listening will vary with our current state of mind and soul. It will also be affected by who we are (in our gifts for listening) and what we are listening to. It is surely affected by the nature of our relationship with the speaker.

It is helpful once again to be clear about our need for self-awareness to inform us when we begin to tire (I don't mean getting bored, because that is another issue). Setting time limits can help us avoid getting to that fade-out point. At times it could be necessary to interrupt the speaker to call a time limit. It is better to set a time limit when you begin, so the speaker has some idea of what time is available. In listening, it is better to give the speaker one's full attention during a limited time period than to give limited listening during an unlimited time period.

Listening time is also limited by the other requirements of doing ministry. While listening participates in every dimension of ministry, it is not *all* of ministry. Sermon preparation and program planning rely on listening, but are demanding functions of ministry apart from listening. The pastor's schedule, as it includes listening, also leaves time for these and other necessary tasks of ministry.

Listening is limited by the setting as well. It is inappropriate for a speaker to begin to pour out deeply felt issues after the service at the door of the sanctuary with other parishioners and visitors standing nearby— they will regret it later. It is the pastor's responsibility to protect the speaker here as well as in other ways we address. Depending on the emotional state of the parishioner, there are at least two options that will protect the parishioner's privacy and provide for the needed listening. One alternative is to walk away with the speaker and find privacy so that you will be able to listen. The other alternative is to quickly arrange for a meeting time with the person to have a longer conversation. These options are set in the context that includes awareness of the pastor's role on Sunday mornings. The listening pastor is in charge of making the setting and the time appropriate to the listening—appropriate for the speaker and for the pastor as well.

Limits of Confidentiality

What does keeping confidentiality mean for a pastor? Confidentiality means that we are not to tell others what has been told to us in confidence. When we are entrusted with the very heart of the lives of speakers, we must hold what we hear with deepest respect. We might think of it as holding what we hear in trust.

Some pastors have considered it safe in terms of confidentiality to share what they have heard in confidence with their spouses. Even though this seems to give pastors a way to unburden, such sharing of what parishioners have told the pastor in confidence is unacceptable. It is unethical to discuss with one's spouse the troubles of those who have sought your help as pastor. The spouse is not bound by professional ethics, as is the pastor.

Too often pastors use what has been entrusted to them in confidence to illustrate a point in a sermon. Of course, no names are used, but that does not mean that the story's subject cannot be identified. Thinking there is safety in using a story because one has been relocated to a different congregation in a distant geographical area is false assurance. We never know who is going to be connected to whom and be able to immediately identify the persons in the illustration.

It can be appropriate to tell a story given in confidence when you have sought and received permission to do so and explicitly say that permission has been given to use the story. Even when permission is given, listeners to the sermon may be cautioned by the telling of another's story and resolve not to talk with the pastor about anything private and important. This problem is resolved by clearly stating that permission to use the story was granted.

When assuring speakers/parishioners of confidentiality, pastors should always offer a disclaimer: When someone is a danger to themselves or to others, I will not promise to keep confidentiality. Also, check with your state laws to make sure you know the legal limits of confidentiality.

When You Are in Over Your Head

The expression "in over your head" originates in the context of swimming. If you are a novice swimmer you need to avoid getting in over your head in the water. More experienced swimmers can go into deeper water safely. Using this expression in regard to listening has similar implications. Levels of experience in listening may allow one to go into deeper listening waters than one whose experience is more limited. The parallel between swimming and listening continues in that even seasoned swimmers recognize when not to go into deeper waters. For them danger has not disappeared with their experience, but continues to pose some limits on where they can go and when. Swimmers may not know immediately that they are in over their heads. The presumption is that the bottom of solid footing is "right there," when suddenly the swimmer notices that it is gone. So, too, in listening; we can end up in over our heads before we are aware of it.

In listening, being in over one's head is related to different kinds of circumstances. One general category of circumstances is when you are dealing with a problem brought to you that is beyond your skills and experience. Another category is when you face something that is too close to home for you personally. For one's own awareness it is important to recognize whether you are professionally prepared and able to deal with an issue brought to you, or if you are in over your head because the issue touches something unhealed in you, something personal. The answer to this does not particularly change your response to the current speaker, but it does say where you need to go—to seek out more professional training or to seek personal healing. Your answer will make a difference for the next person who comes with a similar issue.

There will be points for every listening pastor at which they will be in over their heads. No one can handle everything. I propose a "four R" method to approach facing over-your-head situations. *The four Rs are recognize, reconnoiter, resource, and refer.* They offer a familiar process for facing difficult moments in listening when we feel a need for some security.

The first R is *recognize*. Recognize that this is where you are (in over your head) and do not deny that you are in over your head. This is a point at which humility and self-awareness are extremely important. We have to be honest with ourselves in order to see when we are in over our heads in dangerous listening waters.

It is easier to try to go a little further or figure out what we can try in order to help the speaker. Swimmers, like listeners, can be tempted to go just a little further out into the water under treacherous circumstances thinking that *maybe* they can handle it. We have more of a tendency to avoid recognizing, because to acknowledge that we are in over our heads feels like failure or incompetence. We have let the speaker down. Maybe that feeling expands to a sense of having let the whole church down.

At the point when we are in over our heads and don't want to recognize it, we may work hard to give folk an answer, to tell them what to do. We may "reach for God" like some pastors who turn to prayer out of desperation, before they have heard the whole story, in order to avoid any more listening. "This is something [praying] I know I can do." Alternatively, pastors also reach for scripture to provide some solid ground when they feel only shifting currents under their feet.[2]

The second R is *reconnoiter*. The pastor's responsibility after recognizing the status of being in over her or his head is to survey the situation, to do an assessment of how it is that this situation is problematic. What put me in over my head? What is it that I am facing that I cannot face and be effec-tive in listening? Here I need to recognize if it is a matter of there being a situation for which I am not professionally prepared by my education or experience or if it is a situation I cannot face because it is touching some-thing too close and painful for me. Here it is necessary for the pastor to evaluate what kind of resources might be needed to face the situation.

The third R is *resource*. As a pastor it is important to know resources available in the immediate and wider geographical areas, and to be famil-iar with other helping persons in the area (and not just look them up in a telephone directory). Prepare yourself by contacting potential resources for referral ahead of time. Clergy associations, area hospitals, and govern-ment agencies are excellent sources for identifying resources that can be useful in a variety of situations. Knowing services such as hospice, respite care, and support groups for specific populations can be valuable when you need them. Visit therapists, counselors, and clinics. Discover their views on religion and what kind of work they do. Be clear that the label "Christian Counselor" does not assure that this is someone who will be the best resource for your parishioners who need to be referred. Know counselors who specialize in particular areas: marriage counseling, sex therapy, sexual abuse, and rape, for example.

Finally, the fourth R is *refer*. Referral is an important option for pastors to be ready to use. Be prepared to make many kinds of referrals before any need for them arises. Being able to make referrals involves being honest with oneself, in self-awareness, and honest with the speaker. The pastoral listener can tell the person, "This is something I cannot help you with. I will be able to find someone who can help." The pastor can enable them to get this help through making telephone calls, going with them to the referral source, and telling them what the referral source will do.

Being able to refer a parishioner demonstrates honest humility and the recognition that no pastor carries total responsibility for meeting the needs of a parishioner. It is not all up to you and you don't have to do it all yourself. Other resources are available for you to work with in the community. Others are there for the people of the church to help you meet their needs. Compassionate self-awareness is helpful at this point. If we cannot offer ourselves compassionate self-awareness we will be con-sistently dissatisfied with what we are able to do. Our humility carries awareness that we live within human limitations. Too often the compas-sion we have for others is not reflected in any compassionate under-standing for ourselves.

A particular example that is likely to come to any pastor, and that very few pastors can handle on their own, is the case of a suicidal person. In this situation we cannot try to resolve what is going on for the speaker when their life is at risk. However, it is important that we enable the person to get to a hospital or to a trusted therapist who is equipped to deal with a threat of suicide. Homicidal threats are to be taken with the same seriousness.

Pastors need information about how to get someone admitted to a hospital. Be aware of the hospital's procedures and its limitations. Usually a hospital admission without the patient's consent will only last a few days for assessment of the person and then, if they choose, the patient is free to go. Someone who poses a danger to others may once again be a threat. Know hospital policies and procedures. Get acquainted with the police and know how to call on them as needed when someone is endangered.

When a pastor makes a referral, the role of the pastor continues as the spiritual guide of the parishioner. No other referral source takes over this part of the healing process, which the person will continue to need. Spiritual guidance does not usurp therapy or support offered by others, but provides an additional source for healing.

Sexual Feelings

It is important in ministry to be able to listen to parishioners talk about sexuality. Talk about sex and sexuality brings us into particular intimacy with the speaker. Many speakers will have uneasiness or embarrassment and feel vulnerable when they bring sexual issues to the listening pastor. The comfort level of the pastor may be easily discerned by speakers and can ease the way or block a conversation about sex. In the context of listening, everyone is vulnerable to inappropriate sexual behavior. The welcoming and receiving that listening involves brings us into difficult territory in which we are wise to beware (be aware).

At the same time that sex is a difficult listening issue, it is clear that we are not sure how much we want to receive or welcome when someone wants to talk about sexual issues. Many issues with which we struggle are located around issues of sex and sexuality. This is surely an area in which we feel most vulnerable and in which we most fear intimacy—as we should.

As we listen to people talk about sexual issues we also have to recognize our own sexual feelings. Here we are *most in need of reliable self-awareness*. Sexual involvement with a parishioner is *never* appropriate, and it may not be a pastor's intention. Sexual involvement usually becomes inappropriate in a step-by-step process moving toward deeper emotional involvement and greater intimacy in touch. Without critical self-awareness, pastors find themselves involved sexually with those who are in their professional care.

Intimacy and vulnerability go hand in hand in inappropriate sexual involvements. To avoid such a hidden danger does not mean to avoid any intimacy, any touch with parishioners. Nor is the answer for the pastor to seek to become entirely invulnerable. Without intimacy and vulnerability effective listening cannot take place. With self-awareness we can allow for intimacy to enter into our listening practice and be able to maintain healthy boundaries.

Pastors deal with the fantasy life of their parishioners whether they want to or not. To some parishioners the pastor is an ideal figure, a powerful leader, and therefore, sexually attractive. (This is entirely independent of how powerful or ideal pastors feel themselves to be.) Gaining the pastor's favor and company creates a sense of power and esteem for the parishioner. Pastors with awareness of this dynamic are less likely to find themselves sexually involved with admiring parishioners. Seeing oneself through the admiring eyes of a persistent other can be very seductive.

To protect ourselves from inappropriate sexual involvements we need unswerving self-awareness and humility, reliable personal relationships, and intimacy with others apart from those in our congregations. Intimate relationships with spouse, partner, family, and friends who fill our needs for intimacy are important. We need people we are able to rely on so we can talk freely about sexual feelings and not have to act upon them.

Issues of sexuality play different roles with various constituencies within the congregation: teens, couples in premarital counseling or care, married couples, those raising children, those with issues of sexual identity, or those with issues of sexual abuse. In addition, throughout life the experience of our sexuality changes and usually people are not ready for recognizing such changes. Some people may struggle because of the expectation that sexuality will remain like it is when we are young adults. In all of these areas people often need someone to talk to. Many parishioners wouldn't ever think of speaking to their pastor about sexual issues; and many pastors are not prepared for this kind of listening, but it is an urgent need among the people of God.

With every group, at all points in life, pastors will need to be able to listen to talk about sex with some degree of comfort, with a sufficient amount of accurate information, and without shame. When the pastor cannot deal with sex comfortably, the pastor's discomfort reinforces shameful feelings about sex that so many of us carry. Listening with *informed comfort* and thoughtful availability is essential.

Some of the sexual issues that people face and may bring to you to listen to include: rape, incest, extramarital and premarital intercourse, teen pregnancies, abortion (before and after), HIV, homosexuality, transsexuality and bisexuality, and sexuality in old age. Each of us has areas with which we struggle and to which we would find it more difficult to listen. We need to be honest with ourselves about where we struggle and cannot listen well; then make a decision about whether we will choose to work toward feeling more at ease in areas with which we are not comfortable. This is a matter of putting oneself in the service of the people. Being there to offer them listening on crucial life issues means we are required to be as ready to be open to listen as we can be.

Sexuality is also an area in which we are likely to carry a lot of judgment. When we feel judgmental about issues that a speaker brings to us, that judgment stands in the way of our welcoming and receiving the speaker in listening. Judgment becomes a barrier to our being present in thoughtful availability to the speaker. Judgment comes out of a position that is invulnerable. Hospitality seems to be absent from judgment.

Jesus' teaching on judging others is quite clear:

> Do not judge, so that you may not be judged. For with the judgment you make you will be judged, and the measure you give will be the measure you get. (Matt. 7:1-2)

> Do not judge, and you will not be judged; do not condemn, and you will not be condemned. Forgive, and you will be forgiven; give, and it will be given to you. A good measure, pressed down, shaken together, running over, will be put into your lap; for the measure you give will be the measure you get back. (Luke 6:37-38)

This is not to say that all sexual behaviors are healthy; it simply means that our ability to be available to speakers who bring us difficult issues can be severely limited when we have presented judgment on those same issues in a sermon or lesson to the congregation.

In the context of considering sexuality in relation to vulnerability in ministry, it may be appropriate to raise the issue of how important it is for some parishioners to have the availability of both female and male ministers from which to choose to meet their needs for being heard. Because of the difference of our gender experiences and socialized perceptions of ourselves and those of the other gender, some parishioners may feel constrained to speak to a woman rather than a man in ministry. It may be in areas related to the very vulnerable topic of sexuality that this is most likely to occur, but such needs are not limited to the area of sexuality.

Barriers We Install to Protect Us from Listening

Pastors have time-honored ways to avoid having to listen to some issues. Probably the most effective may be to preach judgmental sermons about an issue you want to avoid hearing about. If you cannot stand the thought of listening to someone talk about abortion or homosexuality, for example, then preaching a judgmental sermon about these issues will eliminate the possibility almost entirely.

Similarly, it is also possible to take a passive approach in which you never speak about an issue, never show any awareness of it—issues such as child abuse, alcoholism, the use of corporal punishment with children, or domestic violence. The likelihood of parishioners bringing these issues to you will be greatly diminished. One pastor reported that the mere mention that he was attending a workshop on battering brought several women from his congregation to talk about their experiences. Prior to that time, he had no idea that they had been battered. That was all it took, just an announcement of a workshop. From this announcement, the women felt their pastor would be prepared to hear them.

We can manage to communicate to the people that we do not want to hear about some issues. This is a good idea *when we are not prepared* to listen to them. Once people get a signal that their pastor will listen to a difficult issue, they will come. It is, however, best that they not be encouraged to come when their pastor is not prepared to face their issue.

The pastor can cultivate an environment in which people feel free to come with any issue. Such an environment can be created when the pastor identifies issues with which she or he is uneasy or feels uninformed and then sets out a personal program to become informed and work toward being able to comfortably listen to talk about the issue from an *informed* perspective. The pastor seeking to create such an environment can also preach and arrange for adult education on the topic, as one church did on AIDS. Previous judgmental views of persons with AIDS were challenged with an educational program offered at the church. Attitudes and views changed.

Can I Believe What I Hear?

Some things that are said are very difficult to believe. We do not want to be made a fool of by trusting that what has been said is true (another dimension of vulnerability) when we suspect or are convinced that it *cannot* be true. *Anything* may be brought to you as a listening pastor, even what you cannot imagine. Can you believe everything that you are told? Should you? It is guaranteed that some truly unbelievable things will be brought to you to hear. This reality presents issues of vulnerability in listening.

Among the issues that could come to the pastor are issues that involve incredible abuse and violence—in particular, abuse reported by the child or the spouse of a valued church member. Abuse of elderly family members by members of the family or by caregivers in their homes or in nursing facilities may seem unbelievable, and yet such incidents are not uncommon.

Reports of rape have often been dismissed as not credible. Women have experienced being blamed for being raped and for being battered by their husbands or lovers. There is a long tradition of questioning the validity of rape claims made by women. At least one in three women and one in six males are likely to experience sexual abuse by the time they are eighteen. The greatest threat to the life of pregnant women in America is becoming victims of homicide committed by their husbands or boyfriends.

Trish

The fourteen-year-old daughter of one of the core leaders of the congregation comes to you and, through her tears, you hear her tell stories of having been sexually abused by her father—that same man who is an esteemed church member and community leader, someone with whom you have worked closely over a number of years. You have seen Trish grow up in the church in the context of her family. You baptized her. She has been a near-perfect student. You have seen no sign that would support what she is saying to you.

As you listen, is your self-awareness alert? Are you aware of your own vulnerability in this circumstance? Do you wish she hadn't come to you? Do you wonder whether she is telling you the truth? How much do you know about the statistics regarding sexual abuse and incest? How much do you know about patterns and behaviors of sexual abuse victims and perpetrators? The degree to which you are informed will determine, to some extent, how you see Trish's situation.

Are you required by the laws of your state to report to the legal authorities that she came in and reported this incident to you?

Al

Another church member comes to you. Al and his family have been part of the congregation since before you came as pastor. It has seemed that his family is picture perfect. He and his wife are responsible and loving parents. The children seem to be growing up into good young adults. You were a bit puzzled when Al asked to speak to you. You had heard what you interpreted as concern in his voice. Al talks a little about his childhood and then broaches the real issue.

Throughout his life, Al has felt like he was a female born in the wrong body. He remembers from childhood feeling like he really was a girl and not a boy, resisting boys' activities and gravitating toward the arts and domestic matters. His work as an architect expresses his artistic interests. He is an excellent cook. He wants to undergo a sex-change process and surgery.[3] Be aware of your feelings. What is your focus? Keep your self-awareness alert. What is Al expecting of you? What role does he want you to play as listener and pastor?

What Can You Expect of Yourself?

In these two scenarios the listening pastor is faced with incredible stories. The occasions are clearly moments of feeling vulnerable for the pastor. They are also moments of doubt and possibly judgment. These are scary issues to deal with in the abstract. In these two cases, though, the pastor considers the families and the community context as well as the individual pains and struggles of Trish and Al. These two scenarios may present the greatest of listening challenges.

Remember that in your listening role as pastor that Trish's father and mother and Al's wife and children are also under your care. What can you expect of yourself in these very difficult situations? When you hear their stories, what does it mean that you will do? What are Trish and Al wanting you to do? Recalling the characteristics of listening that have been discussed: Will you be able to provide thoughtful availability, be willing to be vulnerable, and be able to continue in humility and self-awareness while listening to these stories?

Trish has told you about her experience of incest with her father. How much do you know about the frequency of sexual abuse of children?[4] Being aware of the frequency of child sexual abuse and understanding who abusers are may make Trish's story more credible. Your starting point is to *believe what is brought to you*. Your position might be something like "innocent until proved guilty," as found in our legal system. Trust what is told to you until you have credible evidence to the contrary. This trust involves a lot of vulnerability for the listener.

You may, however, think that you already have enough credible evidence that Trish is *not* telling the truth. You *know* her father! You *know* the family! The whole community knows them! What can you do with what she has told you? You have seen no signs of abuse—that you know of. You may feel defensive for Trish's father, for the church community, for yourself.

Let's think briefly about Trish and Al in light of the four Rs that I have recommended. I suggest their use here because these two situations are likely to feel beyond most pastors' abilities. If pastors who listen to Trish and Al do not have information about either sexual abuse of children or transsexual experiences, these two situations are likely to be overwhelming. Pastors are likely to have strong feelings about having to be able to deal with these situations, which may make it difficult to recognize that they are in deep listening water. These situations can easily make pastors feel defensive for themselves and for the church. What does hearing these two people say about who we are as a church and who I am as a pastor? We see right away that the first R of *recognizing* will be difficult.

In the process of *reconnoitering* these situations, pastors may clearly recognize that they are in over their heads. They then have to assess how it is that this situation is problematic. It may seem obvious. "I never thought I would have either a transsexual or a child abuser in my church. How could I have been prepared for this?" In these situations it is doubtful that there will be a clear-cut distinction between whether it is our feelings or our lack of preparation for either of these situations that has thrown us into deep water. The reconnoitering assessment can still be helpful. It will help pastors look at their interconnections with these situations.

What resources am I aware of that would be helpful in these situations? This takes me to the third R, *resource*. If pastors do not prepare ahead of time, this is a point at which they may really feel under water. "Who can help me understand these situations, either of them? Where can I look for help?" Pastors should know whether they are required by law to report sexual abuse of children. But this does not give the answers pastors will need. Pastors would have to go further with Trish and Al to discover what they were looking for in speaking out. Since Trish is a minor and her abuser is in her home, she will need to be protected from further abuse. The pastor will need to contact Trish's mother. How does Trish feel about that? Her mother could be a great resource or could complicate the problem with denial.

Referral, the fourth R, depends on understanding more of what Al wants from the pastor. Has Al worked out support and psychological and medical consultations? Is he in the process of transition? What is happening in his relationship with his wife? If Al is looking for someone to walk with him on the spiritual side of his journey, referral may not be appropriate, unless at the reconnoiter stage the pastor discovered that her or his feelings were so strong regarding transsexuals that it would be impossible to walk with Al through the next steps of his life. Referral would be necessary if Al were just at the beginning of exploring the possibility of taking this traumatic life step. Al would need many experts whose experience and training are far beyond what the pastor could bring. Trish would need a referral to an expert in dealing with child sexual abuse.

Whether or not you believe what has been said, you still want to be a good listener. Other factors may impinge on your role. In some states law mandates that the clergy, along with teachers, doctors, and counselors, must report any cases of child sexual abuse brought to them. Be sure that you know the laws of your state. Your role as listener remains primary. Neither of these issues, Al's or Trish's, are matters you can deal with on your own. You might have to report Trish's situation to authorities. For Al, you would want to be sure that he will be supported through his decision by competent and caring professionals. (Al did not come to you for help to *decide*.) Your focus on the spiritual lives of Trish and Al and their families is crucial. What are their current struggles with their faith in light of their life experiences? This is not likely to be a question you would ask any of the persons involved. This question can be held as a focus for your concern and care for each family member in these two situations.

With these two extremely difficult and complicated situations it may be necessary for pastors involved to get some referrals for themselves. When pastors do not have information and exposure to such issues, it will be necessary to seek out ways to grow in these areas. Where can pastors go for more information, for greater understanding of the experiences that Trish and Al have shared? This is part of the listening responsibility of the pastor.

The fact that Trish and Al came to you with their difficult stories says something about you as a listening pastor. There was something—some level of trust and listening—thoughtful availability, perhaps, which opened the door for them to choose to come and speak to you.

Vulnerability in Conflict

Up to this point, the focus of listening has been on one-to-one listener-speaker relationships, but listening is also a crucial function of ministry in the context of groups of people. Conflict in the church is one issue that calls for the best of listening and calls out the most painful of vulnerabilities. At this point we will look at conflict in relation to the vulnerability necessary for listening in conflict. In the next chapter we will return to conflict in its community context, seeing the importance of reciprocity in listening with more attention to the community's role in reciprocity.

The church is no stranger to conflict. From the earliest days of the church, events recorded in the New Testament demonstrate that church founders and leaders struggled with the church in conflict.[5] Today conflict within churches causes enormous damage to the church community, individuals in the church, and pastors. Listening well provides the possibility for dealing with conflict in constructive ways. Church splits may produce church plants, but they also produce much pain and strife, which can reverberate for years (and decades).

All that we have explored about listening coalesces in listening in the midst of conflict: self-awareness and humility; body language and all other forms of nonword communication; willingness to be vulnerable and the strength and courage necessary for all of this. Issues that cause and escalate conflict are those centered in deep and differing values—issues with strong feelings attached to them. Listening skills are put to the test in such emotionally charged situations. In the next chapter, as we deal with mutuality in listening, we will examine more fully the role of listening in dealing with conflict. We notice here that being present to conflict may be the point at which we feel most vulnerable.

Conclusion

We have been exploring the many ways in which the listener is vulnerable when truly listening. This chapter surely does not cover all of the possible ways in which listeners experience vulnerability. The unexpected, the challenging, the unknown catch us off guard as listeners. We also discover that what comes to us in the person of the speaker, like the guest who arrives unexpectedly, brings into our lives both the potential for danger and the potential for change. We have seen some of the dangers as well as potentials for change. In many ways listening is not only difficult to do well, but it can be uncomfortable when done well. Just as with humility, we found a necessity for courage in listening because of our vulnerability. In the next chapter we will examine the final characteristic of hospitality, which we also find in the practice of effective listening, reciprocity, and its role in listening in a wider context of the community.

Focus Questions/Activities

When have you felt that you were in over your head in a conversation? Did you feel like you were able to resolve the feeling?
Can you identify some issues about which you feel you need more study, preparation, or experience?
What will you do about these needs for your preparation in ministry?

Exercise 4: "Not *That* Issue!"

Introduction: All of us have issues with which we do not want to deal—which we never want to face. This exercise gives you the opportunity to encounter something you would rather not. You begin by selecting the issue you most want to avoid. I will list a few to get you thinking: addiction to pornography, divorce, a child abuser, spouse abuse, elder abuse, sexual orientation, drug or alcohol abuse, infertility, death of a child, birth abnormality, someone who is incarcerated, a transsexual, someone who has been raped, a woman who has had an abortion, a "sexual pervert," someone with Alzheimer's disease, someone with a mental illness. Your issue may not be on this list. After choosing your issue, allow the issue some space in your self, offering it hospitality—a place at your table where you can meet (it need not be a long visit). There could be a gift waiting for you somewhere in relation to this issue. Either before or after (or both before *and* after) the exercise below, begin to learn something about the issue you want to avoid. Allow yourself to be open to learn and understand. Reading books, going on the Internet, seeing movies, interviewing people, going where people are whose issues you want to avoid, all can be helpful.

Exercise Set Up: You will need a partner for this exercise who meets two qualifications. (1) Your partner should be someone you feel you can trust; and (2) your partner's issue-I-want-most-to-avoid should be different from your issue. You need someone who may be able to face the issue you cannot face. As usual, find a time period and choose a place where you will not be distracted. (Do I have to say, "Turn off your cell phones"?) You need at least a half an hour—more is better—but agree on your time limits.

For this exercise you are to prepare yourself to bring to your listener the issue you do not want to face. You enter the conversation role-playing as a person who brings to your listener partner the issue you want most to avoid. If you think you do not have such an issue, do some brainstorming with a few classmates or friends. If you find an issue, but do not think your feelings about it are as strong as I have suggested here, go ahead and work with that issue. Look at the list provided above. You might want to do some research to prepare for your role. Remember, if there is an issue you never want to face in ministry, *it is very likely it will come to you* no matter whether you think your place of ministry will be far from that possibility. This is your opportunity to face it in a safe way.

The Exercise: Come to the listener with whom you are working prepared to speak as the person you want to avoid. You are putting yourself in their shoes and trying to discover what they might want to bring to the pastor. Make every effort to be authentic and not a caricature of the person.

The listener has the responsibility to call you on not being faithful to the role. Otherwise the listener performs the listening role as effectively as possible, responding to the person you are role-playing. The listener will also give you feedback following the conversation regarding your faithfulness to the role.

The speaker is to receive what the listener says during the conversation and get a sense of how it feels from the perspective of the role the speaker is playing. "How did it feel [to the role person] when the pastor/listener said . . . ?"

The Written Assignment: The speaker writes a brief narrative of the experience. Be clear in presenting the choice of issue and your present understanding of what made this a difficult issue to face and how you feel about it after the exercise. Evaluate your ability to play the role and include reflection on your reactions to the listener's responses to your role person. Go over the paper with your listener for more feedback. Again, there may be material here you will want to include in your listening journal.

CHAPTER FIVE

LISTENING FOR THE VOICE OF GOD: RECIPROCITY IN LISTENING

Introduction

We have seen reciprocity as one of the core qualities of hospitality. In hospitality we may or may not have begun with an image of guest and host as truly reciprocal. Reciprocity goes beyond the usual giving and receiving in hospitality and in listening. The surprising reciprocity in the turnaround of guest becoming host and host becoming guest (which may happen more than once in a given story) was found in each scripture that we explored. From the one who comes in need, the one who meets the need unexpectedly receives gifts.

In chapter 4, "Listener Beware," we recognized many points at which the listener needs to exercise caution and we realized the burden that listening can become. In this chapter on reciprocity in listening, we begin to see what we might discover as the joy of listening. We witness the joy of seeing the speaker "get it," and we come away from the listening with joy of our own.

Reciprocity tends to come as a by-product of listening done well and is not inherent in the act of listening itself. Reciprocity represents the joy part of the hard work of listening, the powerful recognition of our being one as we share a common humanity—a humanity in which we share in the joy as well as the suffering of human experience. The joy also comes in the recognition that you and I are us and we in God, for we share in common our being created in the image of God.

As we have noticed in the scripture stories, whereas the guests are seen as the ones who are in need, their need does not preclude their host's receiving a gift. Guests who come in need of hospitality give extraordinary gifts before they leave. The gifts given are not tangible, but may be simply a reconfirmation of a promise or as much as saving the host's life. At times, the gifts come in the form of reminders of what is already possessed by the host, like the promise Abraham had received from God and like the forgiveness the woman at Simon's house had already received. Speakers, like guests, do not necessarily know at the start what they bring to their hosts.

The discovery that Jesus becomes our guest when we offer hospitality to "the least of these" is an expression of this reciprocity. Our hospitality shown to those in need is actually hospitality extended to Jesus. From offers of hospitality to "the least of these," the one who stands in for the guests rewards us. In the experience of reciprocity, hospitality extended by us to those in need becomes hospitality returned to us from Jesus.[1]

In addition, the Letter to the Hebrews tells us that when we receive someone (as in hospitality and in listening), we do so with the sense that we suffer *as though* we are in their place—again, a sense of reciprocity. What is theirs I experience *as though* it is mine in terms of suffering, pain, torture, hunger, loss. Be clear, as a listener, that you *do not feel the pain of the speaker.* "As though" gives us some distance from their pain and allows them to continue in ownership of their feelings.

As with hospitality, at the beginning we may find it difficult to see reciprocity in listening when it is clear there is a listener who is host to the speaker who is in need as the guest. We may begin by seeing listening as an image of one person doing the speaking (the one who is the guest and receiver) and another listening (the one who is the host and giver). This image does not appear to be reflective of reciprocity. However, in listening, the roles reverse from time to time as the speaking changes hands and roles change within the action.

In some contexts, the listening role may have the effect of seeming to support nonreciprocity. It may be that some people see ministry as service only from the minister to the congregation. The pastor is host and the people are guests; the people come with needs and the pastor meets their needs. The pastor, for some churchgoers and members, may not be seen as a person who has needs. The pastor brings God to the people, and the people to God. The people do not bring God to the pastor, or the pastor to God. Reciprocity belies all of this.

In the model of nonreciprocal, one-directional ministry, the pastor remains the host throughout the relationship; the people remain the guests. But we have learned that neither hospitality nor listening function in ways that keep the participants in their same roles. Hospitality teaches us something else. There are reversals and turnarounds. The movement is back and forth, exchange and counterexchange. The guest-host relationship does not remain static and neither does the speaker-listener relationship.

In the midst of listening to a guest, I may also find myself receiving God's hospitality. In some cases, God's word can come to me through the revelations of another person without that person's intention or awareness. God becomes the acting host and I become a guest alongside the one who has been speaking as guest to me. Reciprocity seems to be something we are more likely to *discover* in the midst of listening, rather than something we are clear about having as we approach listening and begin to listen.

In this chapter we move to explore some wider contexts for listening as we see the role of listening and reciprocity in community. Whereas reciprocity functions in one-to-one listening relationships, it also takes a major role within listening communities and groups.

Reciprocity in Our Shared Humanity

Reciprocity has its roots in our common humanity—in what we share with all other human beings. Our common ground of shared humanity first is found in our being *created in the image of God*. Every one of us carries the image of God and shares in this image with all other human beings. Second, in our commonly shared humanity is the reality that *all of us are sinners*. We all fall short. Finally, *all of us have in common the human experiences of pain, suffering, fear, loss, and joy—every human emotion*.

The fact that all suffer and all experience joy gives us avenues for understanding one another, but our own experiences do not reveal to us what another's experiences are like. We have to rely on the other to tell us. For an understanding of others' experiences I need to hear the particulars of *their* lives. We have so much in common when we view one another in light of our common humanity. What is different about us is important, but it is never the whole or most important part of the picture of our lives. When we focus entirely on what we do not have in common our differences become barriers between us, and impediments to being able to truly listen to the other.

In many cases, it is the strangeness of the other—what is unfamiliar to us—that creates barriers. Listening is an avenue to overcoming this strangeness, as we remain open to learn, and grow in understanding the other person's life. A male friend described an experience of being in a situation in which a group of women were freely speaking with one another. (Keep in mind that this man has been married for many years. He has not been isolated.) He reported having no idea that women spoke with such candor and humor together. His experience of hearing a group of women speaking freely, having forgotten there was a man in the room, was very revealing to him.

This occasion would have offered a wonderful opportunity for the man to have entered into dialogue with the women, with humility, to learn more about the women's concerns, joys, and worries. When the women discovered that this man was so surprised by their conversation, it could have been a good opportunity for them to discover how unknown they are to the men in their lives.

Our Common Humanity in a Multicultural Context

Recognition of our common humanity as inclusive of our being created in the image of God—all of us being sinners and all of us sharing the basic human experiences of sorrow, pain, loss, fear, and joy—is helpful in our effective listening. However, those of us who are members of the predominant cultural group of European Americans may tend to extend our understanding of our common humanity to include particularities of our cultural assumptions as part of our understanding of what our common humanity means. These assumptions mean that we ignore or are not aware of cultural differences within our humanity. We cannot add on to our understanding of common humanity assumptions, which are entirely shaped by our culture, about how speaking and listening ought to be.

Many Americans listen from a Eurocentric standpoint, their listening limited by cultural context. Persons of other cultures and races throughout much of the world grow up knowing us in ways we never get to know them, because our culture surrounds them and impinges on their own cultures. To give a simple example of a very complex situation: young South African theological students listen over and over to tapes of American preachers. Do any of us hear tapes of their preaching? Beyond hearing quotes from Bishop Tutu, I think we remain isolated.

We cannot listen effectively across cultures without humility. We cannot listen effectively across cultures hoping to remain unchanged or being unwilling to change. We hold our common humanity as a starting point from which we can accumulate further understanding of others, beyond our cultural differences.

Our Shared Humanity and Jesus

We further consider our shared humanity by returning to the Scripture's account of Jesus washing the feet of the disciples (John 13:3-8). In chapter 2, we could see that Jesus was willing to demonstrate humility with his disciples and challenge a concept like "once the host always the host," which would hold Jesus in an elevated position of teacher and Lord. In the context of reciprocity we understand that what he called for from the disciples was that sense of exchange and a shifting between host and guest, calling forth from them servantship to one another. Jesus demonstrated his being part of the common humanity of the disciples in his action of washing the disciples' feet. He was one with them, and told them that his action was to be emulated by them with one another.

We may experience uneasiness with reciprocity, feeling a sense of resistance to it because the turnaround of reciprocity is usually unexpected. Reciprocity does not allow things to stay where they were. Jesus, Lord and teacher, acted as servant to the disciples. We see how difficult it was for Peter to accept that Jesus would take on this role,[2] which gives us a clue as to how powerful the message of this reversal in reciprocity was for the disciples—*their Lord washing their feet!* I doubt if we can assume that all the other disciples felt comfortable with Jesus washing their feet. To his actions Jesus added instructions that the disciples were to do likewise, encouraging them to continue in reciprocity.

What I see underlying this experience between Jesus and the disciples is potential for joy. Here was their leader, their Lord, their teacher, and he was on his knees honoring them by washing their feet himself. This was not a traditional role for a Lord or teacher. In these actions with the disciples, Jesus continued his way of defying the divisions between people, showing the disciples that there was no barrier defining him as apart from or above the role of servant to others. His action affirmed reciprocity among them and in their ministry.

Joy for the disciples also could be found in how their view of themselves could be changed by this event. Reciprocity has a way of enabling guests/speakers to see themselves in a different light. Once they could get past their discomfort with the reversal Jesus initiated—their disease with reciprocity—joy could be available to them. Jesus serving them in reciprocity reveals something about their relationships with one another and their identity as servants with a servant God. They could see that if they were worthy of Jesus washing their feet—serving them—then they were *truly* worthy.

As listeners, we usually don't find reciprocal reversals to be as comfortable for us as they were for Jesus. We have to intentionally seek to overcome our uneasiness with participating in reciprocity.

Listening in Faith

Listening in faith requires approaching listening with openness to hear and receive, with the recognition that reciprocity may become part of the picture. Listening in faith includes listening for the voice of God as I listen to another person. Listening in faith requires what we have recognized as the need to listen with thoughtful availability; it requires courage to be humble, vulnerable, and open to the unexpected and to change. Listening in faith is done with awareness that God is going to show up. We recognize that God is a change agent in our lives and in the lives of others and that God's ways of communicating with us are not limited by our expectations or by our previous experience. We continue in our consideration of listening in faith by seeing its value in some particular dimensions of listening.

Listening in Faith for the Voice of God

When we want to hear God we prepare ourselves to be open and to receive, to be available to whatever God has for us. But usually in prayer we bring so much to say to God. Even in silent prayer we are the ones doing the speaking to God. Our difficulties in being silent with one another are also real in our prayer lives. I have witnessed moments of silent prayer in public worship that last no more than one minute. It is hard for us to be open to hear God, so we don't leave much listening space. Throughout the ages, being open to what God had to say has been difficult. "You want me to do *what?*" Prayer is not intended to be a mono-logue, but is meant to be a dialogue, with God speaking as well as listen-ing. Listening for the voice of God requires listening in faith.

Listening for the voice of God also requires us to be open to the unex-pected. God has unlimited ways of reaching out to us, but we can limit what we will hear in our fear. When our listening comes out of faith, we listen with awareness that God does have something for us.

Listening in Faith to the Voice of the Congregation

A priority for beginning to enter into ministry in a new congregation is to *go and listen.* Any approach to listening to the congregation comes out of listening in faith—expecting to hear what will help me understand this congregation and expecting to hear what will enable me to truly become the pastor they need. The reciprocal nature of this listening lies in my becoming the guest to the stories and to the people in order to become their pastor. Through their words and stories I fully expect to fur-ther come to understand what God has called me here to do.

Every congregation has history and stories. Even an apparently uneventful history holds rich information for an incoming pastor. What events and people have shaped the life of this church? What have been the traumatic events in the life of the congregation? What do the people value about this particular community of faith? What do you think is important for me to know about this church? What are your most trea-sured memories of the church? Is there anything you remember that you wish hadn't happened?

As pastors enter new positions in unfamiliar communities and congre-gations, their role as hosts to the people already present comes in the form of receiving them by listening to their stories. Longtime members, more recent members, active and inactive members (even former members), all will be sources for understanding underlying dynamics of the congregation.

The reciprocity in this listening comes as pastors function as hosts to the speaking members and then discover themselves as guests to the stories of the congregation because they are new in this place.

The pastor, who has come to serve a congregation and goes to listen to the people in order to understand them and the ministry they need, initiates a process of reciprocity. The pastor who comes as host to the congregation is the guest in listening to the people. Gifts of understanding from this listening process may serve pastors well for years to come.

Listening in Faith When We Don't Want to Hear

In chapter 4 we looked briefly at conflict as an experience of vulnerability. Let us return to the issue of conflict, thinking about it in the context of reciprocity. We return to a deeper look at listening in conflict situations.

We are enabled to listen in the presence of alienation and conflict when we listen in faith. Even here, in the midst of strife of any kind, we can expect a word from God. I believe that the differences we have do not have to divide. I believe that, with effective listening, that which divides can be diminished and that which we hold in common can be nourished in growth. Otherwise, when I don't believe these things—which means I don't listen in faith—then I will hear only that which will help me shape my next point of argument. I will avoid listening. Without faith, I cannot listen in moments of conflict and alienation.

A recent listening workshop that I attended included people with widely diverse and strongly held views on human sexuality.[3] We were gathered together voluntarily to listen to one another. Participants were seated at round tables and encouraged to speak to those around their table—each out of her or his own experience and faith, addressing their own personal views on human sexuality and their personal experiences with sexuality. Participants were expected to listen to others respectfully (much like the listening described in this book). Speaking was not to be done in reaction to what others said.

Speaking was voluntary and measures were taken to be certain that all who wanted to speak had an opportunity. As people around the table took turns speaking, it was apparent that those gathered there were, indeed, very diverse in both their views and their experiences. Responses by listeners were limited to comments such as, "Help me to see better your point of view." No questions or judgments were allowed. Feelings were strong for all those gathered around the table and present in the workshop. Some participants were amazingly open in what they shared at the table. I presumed that similar scenarios were taking place at the other tables around the room. When we had all had a chance to speak and be heard, we were given an opportunity to take time to prayerfully consider the experience and all that we had heard and shared.

Next we were asked to share what we considered to be common values informing our ministries. This took place in more of a discussion format. In each of the segments of this workshop participants were instructed to take some time in silence to think about what they wanted to say. In this way, as in the first part of the workshop, we prepared ourselves before we spoke and did not rely on what others said as prompting our responses.

Whereas the first part of the workshop revealed great differences in our views, amazingly we found during the second part that we had a great deal that we enthusiastically held in common in our views of human sexuality. The table of diverse people created a list of values on which we all were in agreement—a list of important values. We were able to find common ground for all of us. We did this work together, reciprocally, through speaking and listening.[4]

The values that divided us were no longer in the foreground. The strength of values on which we could agree became more important. I have never been more convinced of the power of listening. When we are in the midst of conflict and we truly listen to one another, *even before we have found common ground*, we are *receiving* those whom we might otherwise perceive as our "enemies." The exchange that moves back and forth as we listen and speak reveals our common ground. The difficulty we may experience of feeling danger from others can only be faced down by listening in faith.

Finding our common ground came through listening to one another with thoughtful availability. Out of our process in which each person took turns at being both guest and host came an experience that demonstrated reciprocity in listening. What we hold in common is far more powerful than what separates us.

Here we have looked at a situation in which differing values had fomented conflict. It is helpful in listening to be aware that values underlie a great deal of that to which we listen. Discovery of the values enables us to respond with greater clarity to what we hear. Noticing values as we hear them is helpful for speakers when they themselves may not have identified the values they are expressing. When we focus exclusively on what is different, we fail to see and, therefore, deny all that we have in common in our humanity.

A number of years ago singer Holly Near sang about unity. She captured the sense of unity in singing, "Unity doesn't always mean agreement. Doesn't ever mean the same."[5] We can't listen in areas where disagreements exist or where we suspect they exist when there are prohibitions on speaking about the issues. "Polite society" is seen by some as prohibiting discussions of religion and politics (perhaps sex didn't make this traditional list because it was so clearly prohibited as a topic for public conversation). In these days when divisions in views seem to be growing ever wider, surely this maxim should be followed: "Don't talk about things about which we don't agree." We feel the danger and threat present in disagreeing that keeps us away from these risky topics.

I grew up in a household in which there were clear prohibitions on discussing certain topics. My mother was in charge of monitoring our discussions and maintaining the prohibitions. There was a system in place by which we were warned to "change the subject." Mother kept an old school bell by the dining room table. When a forbidden topic came up and we launched into debate, she was quick to ring the bell, signaling a necessity to shift the conversation. After a number of years, we would automatically call out, "Ring the bell!" when we recognized we were on conflicted ground. The bell itself was no longer necessary. I doubt if many families have a process that is so blatant, but most of us have learned to avoid speaking about topics that are prohibited.

Listening in faith will not do us much good in an atmosphere in which we feel compelled to avoid speaking on certain topics. The listening workshop described above created space for us to talk together on the difficult topic of sexuality. Many people have not had this kind of opportunity for speaking and listening. Our job as listening pastors, then, extends to discovering ways in which we can create an atmosphere in which speaking on disagreeable topics *can* take place. The characteristics of hospitality and listening discussed in this book can provide some ways to understand what such space would require.

Discussions of topics on which we are likely to find disagreement are seldom done with humility and self-awareness. When we engage in these topics we do experience vulnerability, but our efforts are to avoid feeling vulnerable rather than see it as an avenue to better communication. Thoughtful availability also seems absent when we discuss difficult issues. Imagine what our presence could be in the midst of conflict when we bring thoughtful availability, humility, and self-awareness; when we are willing to be vulnerable and expect reciprocity within and following our communication. Listening in faith is essential. Isn't all of this what we are called to be and do?

Empathy as Reciprocity

Hebrews offers us the challenge: "Remember those who are in prison, *as though* you were in prison with them; those who are being tortured, *as though* you yourselves were being tortured" (Hebrews 13:3). We might understand what is said here as *having empathy* with those who suffer. In empathy we join with those who are in need without taking over for them in experiencing their need.

"As though" expresses the experience of reciprocity with them in a way that may help us see something of the boundaries of reciprocity—"as though" helps us keep ourselves separate even as we join in recognizing our common humanity. "As though" gives us a key to recognizing boundaries to empathy. We *do not experience the feelings of the speaker*, but from our common humanity we recognize what speakers feel and join with them in their suffering or joy. We sense what the speaker experiences *as though* we were in the same place, not as we are but *as though* we are in the same place.

"I feel your pain" is not a goal for listening. Nor is it appropriate to say, "I know just how you feel." We do not take over the feelings of the speaker in a way that these phrases imply. Jesus washing feet of disciples broke down barriers in understanding of who he was and who his disciples were. His actions changed their perceptions of themselves. His actions did not change who Jesus was in relation to the disciples. His actions changed the way they saw him in relation to themselves.

Being Changed in Listening

One aspect of vulnerability in listening is the potential of being changed by the listening encounter. Even though change is so imbedded in every aspect of our lives, we still are not comfortable with its prospect. We feel vulnerable in the face of change or in facing the possibility of change. What a speaker brings to the listener may well be something new. We do not know what to expect. Meeting something we never met before in what the speaker says is one aspect of the potential for change we face as listeners.

Change also comes to us when we hear something that is new to us and we make a choice to go and seek more knowledge about the issue we received from the speaker. Our change does not end with the end of the conversation with the speaker, but may continue for some time—even years—as we grapple with what the speaker has given us. When we learn more about issues, our experience of having more information or new information can be transforming in our lives and in our listening.

Reciprocity functions when I discover what I lack at one point and then I set about to change. In meeting an issue with which I am uncomfortable in one person, I respond in learning and growing for being better prepared for another person. My change is for myself and for the other I will later encounter. My change also may become a gift to the congregation as I have grown in understanding and knowledge.

Not long ago, I was giving a lecture. At the conclusion of the lecture I invited questions. There was only one question. The person who asked the question seemed unfriendly and was upset about a particular part of the lecture. Right there in front of a crowd of people, I was (I felt) being called on the carpet for what I did not say. Beyond my fear; beyond my "great internal No!"; beyond my embarrassment; beyond my feelings of inadequacy; beyond the vulnerability I experienced, I recognized the truth in what was said. I knew I had more work to do on the issue identified by the questioner.

While the questioner had been the listener to my speech, I became the listener to the questioner. Reciprocity entered the situation in that I had been the speaker and the questioner had been the listener. Without being willing to be vulnerable, to receive and welcome the question, I would have lost this opportunity for change and growth that was given to me. I continue to struggle and learn about the concern raised by the questioner.

Joy in Reciprocity

The image of joy I hold is of a seminary student, Sam, a former military man, who wept at the recognition that he was precious in God's sight and therefore precious to all of humanity. As his listener, I experienced shared joy with Sam. My joy was found in this experience as the gift of joy coming from God in the midst of his speaking and our listening. God spoke to both of us an affirmation of Sam's preciousness.

The reciprocal gift for me was not only the joy shared with Sam, but my awakening to my own preciousness. But it did not end there. Precious became a part of my prayer life as I prayed for the precious others who inhabit my life and with whom I share classrooms. Precious became an imbedded way of seeing the students I teach. Through that moment with Sam, a piece of my life was transformed by listening to God in listening to Sam. What an incredible gift! Joy that keeps on reverberating, possibly through many lives.

Focus Questions

Recall a situation in which you were transformed by something you heard someone say.

How does it feel to you to be the receiver? To be the giver? Are you more comfortable with one than the other?

Practice sitting quietly in a receptive state, for five minutes each day, for a seven-day sequence. Then answer the question: What have you heard from God lately?

Exercise 5: Taking on a Role

Identify someone who might come to you for your listening skills and yet someone with an issue unlike anything you have experienced before, personally or professionally (infertility, divorce, unemployment, nursing home residency, a debilitating illness are some examples). Do some research to find out what this person's experience may be. Try to find firsthand information, not just information *about* the person. This can be done through reading and interviews, for example. Find places to visit where you could be exposed firsthand to your role person's life.

Now you are prepared to put yourself in this person's shoes. This is an exercise in reciprocity via empathy. What is it like to be this person? How does the issue you have chosen influence different parts of their life? What values do you hold that might shape how you listen to this person?

If this exercise is done in the context of a class, there may be an opportunity to bring this person (you *as* this person) to class to inform others in class about your experience.

Written Assignment: Write about your experience in this role. Include what you would want from someone listening to you. Be explicit. What would be helpful for you as you stand in their shoes and see life from their perspective?

Epilogue

Sometimes what happens on the way somewhere turns out to be as significant as and sometimes more significant than the destination itself. In the case of writing this book I want to affirm that I found it valuable to pay attention to what happened along the way. What happens on the journey is usually unexpected and unanticipated, just like the gifts guests surprisingly left with their hosts in the stories of Abraham and Sarah, Lot, and the gracious woman at Simon's house.

Coming to understand both hospitality and listening in deeper ways has led me back to the classroom where I have spent more than thirty years teaching seminarians. It has also led me to take a look at the church and to consider its leadership provided by the seminaries. Now I take what I have learned from the explorations of this book and the process of writing it and bring it all back to the contexts of theological education and the church.

In the process of writing this book, I discovered the centrality of hospitality in Christian living. What I also discovered (that I already knew) is the transformative power of listening. Listening to others changes the listener. Being heard by another changes the speaker.

I have long thought of transformation as an essential part of theological education. This is true not only for the students but also for those who teach. I expect that every class I teach will change my life in some way. My many years of teaching have not altered this expectation. Ideally, pastors would carry similar expectations—that their ministry to a particular people in a particular place will be an experience of transformation for themselves. What impact would this expectation of the pastor have within the church? How would it change the experience of ministry for pastors?

Because of the transformative potential of theological education, theological seminaries are dangerous places—dangerous because following

Jesus is dangerous. It was dangerous for Jesus to go his way and it is dangerous for every Christian who seeks to follow in doing what Jesus would have us do. Transformation can lead to transgression—transgression of boundaries that divide us in thought, faith, and action.

No less is true for the church, which also is a dangerous place—when it functions at its best. The church following Jesus becomes a place for the kind of outrageous hospitality that the woman offered Jesus at Simon's house (hospitality not particularly appreciated by the religious leaders present). The church is also a setting for transformation. We preach as if that is what we are looking for, but sometimes we find the radical and dangerous transgressing way of Jesus is not exactly where we want to go or where we want to see others go.

Listening has life-giving and life-discovering power. When a person is encouraged to speak and is heard deeply, that person can find their way. Our listening opens doors for their path and leads to the healing of their pains. Listening has the power to transform. This is true in the context of the community of theological education as well as in the context of the church community. Listening also offers the opportunity for us to transcend ourselves as we come to understand another and God from new perspectives discovered in our listening.

In the midst of the settings of theological education and the church, the characteristics of hospitality and listening are bedrock essentials for transformation. Even though we are busy doing many things, uneasy with intimacy and vulnerability, and occasionally hold aversions to humility, we need to face our barriers to receiving others with thoughtful availability if we are to be truly obedient followers of Jesus.

Listening plays a central role at just those points in ministry that pastors may experience as most burdensome. Hearing the pain and grief of parishioners and facing the tension of conflict within the church require of pastors the practice of listening that flows out of the core characteristics discussed in this book.

The effectiveness of listening is not determined by set practices and procedures, but more by the character of the listener. Preparation for ministry that includes both effective listening and warm hospitality is not purely determined by the information gained in theological education. The character of the context for theological education has a powerful effect on the pastors' preparations to meet the struggles of the people with openness and careful listening. What enables institutions of theological education to grow leaders who are able to practice humility's gift of self-awareness and vulnerability's gift of openness to others and to change?

The church stands in need of pastoral leaders who are clearly self-aware, humble, and able to tolerate vulnerability in relation to God and to others. I don't think this is the standard fare of seminary graduates. People who are honestly self-aware and able to tolerate vulnerability are there in seminaries and graduating from seminaries, but they are not in the majority. The church is not always open to these leaders because they tend to make the church more dangerous. They tend to get into the business of enabling the church members to grow in their faith and change from the past limitations of their faith.

How we go about the process of theological education has the possibility to strengthen the listening abilities of the pastors who emerge as leaders for the churches and to enable their ability to provide models for listening and hospitality in the churches. How we go about being the church also has the possibility for transforming our communities of faith.

The church needs pastoral leaders who are able to tolerate honestly looking at themselves and recognizing both their gifts and their limitations. Only then will pastors be able to listen effectively without their own "stuff" getting in the way and demanding that they "fix" the situation. The church needs pastoral leaders who can tolerate the vulnerability experienced in truly listening to another—vulnerability that recognizes that when another is truly heard, the listener is changed as well as the speaker. The church needs pastoral leaders who are able to provide thoughtful availability to those who suffer and to those who rejoice, or moments of transformative listening are lost. The church needs pastoral leaders who can both recognize and receive reciprocity without discomfort and denial.

Many church communities are in pain. Too many are rightly labeled as "toxic." The pain held by these churches is awaiting leadership that can truly welcome and receive the people who suffer within the church. Perhaps it is only a small step toward healing, but I believe that the pastor who comes with the essential characteristics of hospitality and listening brings to churches in pain the means for healing through the power of effective listening.

NOTES

Acknowledgments

1. Michael P. Nichols, *The Lost Art of Listening* (New York: Guilford Press, 1995).

Introduction

1. See for example, Deborah Tannen, *Talking from Nine to Five: How Women's and Men's Conversational Styles Affect Who Gets Heard, Who Gets Credit and What Gets Done at Work* (New York: William Morrow, 1994). Also see her other books: *That's Not What I Meant! How Conversation Style Makes or Breaks Your Relations with Others* and *You Just Don't Understand: Women and Men in Conversation.*

2. Whether the teens using this concept truly grasp the feeling dimension that I am addressing is not clear, but their use of the concept points to an underlying truth.

3. At the conclusion of many parables Jesus said, "Let anyone with ears to hear listen." See Mark 4:9, 7:16; and Luke 8:8, 14:35 for examples. Matthew 7:24-27 includes the importance of action that follows the hearing.

4. "Hearing" (as discussed here) does not exclude the hearing impaired. American Sign Language used by those who are hearing impaired is also subject to the difficulties addressed in this book. The "listener" to sign language still brings to the act of "hearing" limitations that are not related to hearing with the ears, but are similar to the difficulties we all encounter in listening.

5. Carroll Wise, *The Meaning of Pastoral Care* (New York: Harper & Row, 1966), 8.

6. The worst of these signs for me came once when I was preaching and a man sitting near the front of the church held up his pocket watch for me to see while he pointed at it.

1. Listening as Christian Hospitality

1. Dennis E. Groh, *In Between Advents: Biblical and Spiritual Arrivals* (Philadelphia: Fortress Press, 1986), 16-17.

2. Chapter 18 begins, "The LORD appeared to Abraham. . . ." and goes on to refer to "three men." Abraham greets one of the men with, "My lord." In verse 13 "the LORD" speaks to Abraham. Verse 22 refers to one of the men as "LORD," and their conversation

leads one to conclude that Abraham is speaking to God. In chapter 19, verse 1, there is another shift and we read, "The *two* angels came to Sodom" (emphasis mine).

3. Note that this horrible piece of the story is seldom emphasized. Lot's virtue in being hospitable is not diminished by his willingness to offer his virgin daughters to the mob as substitutes for his guests.

4. William R. Herzog II, *Prophet and Teacher: An Introduction to the Historical Jesus* (Louisville: Westminster John Knox Press, 2005), 91.

5. Ibid.

6. Ibid., 93.

7. Ibid., 92.

8. Ibid., 93.

9. Remember to see this question and answer, plus Jesus' following commentary, as of benefit to the crowd and not only as intended for Simon.

10. Sometimes those we think we *do know well* may be the ones to whom we open our homes and hearts in vulnerability without recognizing the risk involved.

11. Groh, *In Between Advents*, 19.

12. Ibid., 19-20.

13. Roland G. Kuhl, "Need for a New Vision of the Pastoral Calling" (unpublished paper, July 20, 2005), 8.

14. See Genesis 19:2-3.

15. Herzog, *Prophet and Teacher*, 93.

16. See Luke 10:29-37.

2. Preparing to Listen

1. Scripture translation is Herzog's. William R. Herzog II, *Prophet and Teacher: An Introduction to the Historical Jesus* (Louisville: Westminster John Knox Press, 2005), 94.

2. Ibid.

3. I know he neither stood up nor shouted, but this is what my feeling reaction was to what the pastor said.

4. In this class every student was invited to become a "role person" for the duration of the class. Roles were drawn from a pile and students were given the option to "get out of" a role that hit too close to home. They then took on the role for a research area and at one point would come to class in that role to talk with the class about their experience. In this way students had opportunities to hear research and experience about a number of issues and, more important, had the opportunity to put themselves into the shoes of another person.

5. Child sexual abuse *is* rape in many cases.

6. For an interesting discussion of this issue see David K. Switzer, *Pastor, Preacher, Person: Developing a Pastoral Ministry in Depth* (Nashville: Abingdon Press, 1979).

7. I have heard one pastor admit this, but I suspect he has thousands of pastor-colleagues who have asked the same question at approximately the same point in a similar conversation.

8. At the time, I was remembering an earlier conversation with Marge in which she was talking about her marriage and family. She was middle-aged and raising teenagers. I was young and had no children. How could I understand? That conversation ended with her

exclaiming, "You have no idea what I am talking about!" The implication was that I was too young and inexperienced. So now I felt under great pressure to convince her that I truly did understand.

3. Listening for What Is Not Being Said

1. Dennis E. Groh, *In Between Advents: Biblical and Spiritual Arrivals* (Philadelphia: Fortress Press, 1986), 20.

2. I had not noticed him doing this before and was astounded that he was behaving in this way. I find myself wondering if he *had* done this before and I had missed it. I wonder if it was using the video equipment, which gave me a vehicle for more attentiveness to Martin's communication. Perhaps focusing on the video camera gave me a new level of awareness.

3. *Presume* is the key word. The listener will probably interpret some meaning to the nonverbal actions but not presume that they are accurate and follow with suggested interpretations to the couple.

4. If you have any doubt about this, watch the fans in the stands at a televised sports event.

5. Myron R. Chartier, *Preaching as Communication: An Interpersonal Perspective* (Nashville: Abingdon Press, 1981), 19.

6. One or two seconds feels like a long time in silence. We usually wait no longer than this to respond.

7. Some persons in ministry do not have a problem hearing the same stories over and over, and are able to lovingly listen and be attentive to the whole telling again and again.

4. Listener Beware

1. Dennis E. Groh, *In Between Advents: Biblical and Spiritual Arrivals* (Philadelphia: Fortress Press, 1986), 16.

2. I am not negating the use of prayer or scripture in listening, but I think both can be abused when their use comes from the pastor's unacknowledged panic of not knowing what to do and the desire that the not knowing remain undiscovered. Under these circumstances neither prayer nor scripture is used to its best advantage.

3. Don't think this can't happen. It has happened to pastors, even in small congregations, with families that seem to be ordinary families.

4. Statistics range that from one in three to one in five girls and one in six to one in ten boys are sexually abused before the age of eighteen. But these statistics may be misleading and researchers suspect there may be higher numbers. See Robert Crooks and Carla Bauer, *Our Sexuality*, 6th ed. (New York: Brooks/Cole, 1996), for a discussion of the complications regarding the available statistics and for an international perspective on the statistics.

5. For example, see 1 Corinthians 1; and Acts 15.

5. Listening for the Voice of God

1. See Matthew 25:35-40.

2. Peter says to Jesus, "You will never wash my feet" (v. 8).

3. Workshop materials noted that it was based on *Common Ground Dialogue*.

4. Our list included: our sexuality is valued as a gift of God; the value of relational integrity and fidelity; belief in the grace and forgiveness of God; identification of many issues we could unite to oppose—sexual abuse, the sex trade, Internet sex, and so forth.

5. Holly Near, "Unity," *Speed of Light*, Redwood Records, 1982.

BIBLIOGRAPHY

Chartier, Myron R. *Preaching as Communication: An Interpersonal Perspective.* Nashville: Abingdon Press, 1981.

Crooks, Robert, and Karla Baur. *Our Sexuality,* 6th ed. New York: Brooks/Cole, 1996.

Ellis, Anne Leo. *First We Must Listen: Living in a Multicultural Society.* New York: Friendship Press, 1996.

Groh, Dennis E. *In Between Advents: Biblical and Spiritual Arrivals.* Philadelphia: Fortress Press, 1986.

Hedahl, Susan K. *Listening Ministry: Rethinking Pastoral Leadership.* Minneapolis: Fortress Press, 2001.

Herzog, William R. II. *Prophet and Teacher: An Introduction to the Historical Jesus.* Louisville: Westminster John Knox Press, 2005.

Hunter, Rodney J., gen. ed. *Dictionary of Pastoral Care and Counseling.* Nashville: Abingdon Press, 1990.

Lindahl, Kay. *Practicing the Sacred Art of Listening: A Guide to Enrich Your Relationships and Kindle Your Spiritual Life.* Woodstock, Vermont: Skylight Paths Publishing, 2003.

Nichols, Michael P. *The Lost Art of Listening.* New York: Guilford Press, 1995.

Ogletree, Thomas W. *Hospitality to the Stranger: Dimensions of Moral Understanding.* Philadelphia: Fortress Press, 1985.

Palmer, Parker J. *The Company of Strangers: Christians and the Renewal of America's Public Life.* New York: Crossroad Publishing, 1983.

Pembroke, Neil. *The Art of Listening: Dialogue, Shame, and Pastoral Care.* Grand Rapids: Eerdmans, 2002.

Rediger, G. Lloyd. *Beyond the Scandals: A Guide to Healthy Sexuality for Clergy.* Minneapolis: Fortress Press, 2003.

Savage, John. *Listening and Caring Skills: A Guide for Groups and Leaders.* Nashville: Abingdon Press, 1996.

Tannen, Deborah. *Talking From Nine to Five: How Women's and Men's Conversational Styles Affect Who Gets Heard, Who Gets Credit, and What Work Gets Done.* New York: William Morrow, 1994.

Volf, Miroslav. *Exclusion and Embrace: A Theological Exploration of Identity, Otherness, and Reconciliation.* Nashville: Abingdon Press, 1996.

Wise, Carroll A. *The Meaning of Pastoral Care.* New York: Harper & Row, 1966.

LaVergne, TN USA
31 March 2011
222255LV00004B/68/P